Warren G. Harding

29th President of
the United States

Warren G. Harding rose from poor and difficult circumstances to become the 29th President of the United States. He believed that American democracy provided all men and women with an equal chance to attain great achievements. (Library of Congress.)

Warren G. Harding

29th President of the United States

Anne Canadeo

GARRETT EDUCATIONAL CORPORATION

Manufactured in the United States of America

Edited and produced by Synthegraphics Corporation

Library of Congress Cataloging in Publication Data

Canadeo, Anne, 1955–
    Warren G. Harding, 29th President of the United States / Anne Canadeo.
        p.   cm. — (Presidents of the United States)
    Includes bibliographical references.
    Summary: Presents the life of Warren G. Harding, including his childhood, education, employment, and political career.
    1. Harding, Warren G. (Warren Gamaliel), 1865–1923 – Juvenile literature.   2. Presidents – United States – Biography – Juvenile literature.   3. United States – Politics and government – 1921–1923 – Juvenile literature.   [1. Harding, Warren G. (Warren Gamaliel), 1865–1923.   2. Presidents.]   I. Title. II. Series.
E786.C38   1990
973.91′4′092 – dc20
[B]
[92]   89-39952
ISBN 0-944483-64-X   CIP
                                                        AC

Contents

Chronology for
Warren G. Harding

1865   Born on November 2 near Blooming
           Grove, Ohio

1879– Attended Ohio Central College in Iberia,
1882   Ohio

1882– Taught school, read law, worked in insur-
1884   ance and on a newspaper

1884   Purchased Marion, Ohio, *Star* with two
           partners

1891   Married Florence Kling De Wolfe on July 8

1895   Lost race for first political office, county
           auditor

1899– Served two terms in the Ohio State
1903   Senate

1904– Served as lieutenant governor of Ohio
1905

1910   Defeated in election for governor of Ohio

1912   Served as chairman of the Republican
           National Convention

1915– Served as United States senator from
1921   Ohio

1921   Inaugurated as 29th President of the
           United States

1923   Died on August 2 in San Francisco

Chapter 1

"An Impossible Candidate"

A n unbearable heat wave had hit Chicago. The temperatures were blistering. The thick, heavy air settled over the city like a cottony blanket. It was the kind of summer Midwesterners call corn weather – good weather for growing things, but not for choosing a President.

Inside the barn-like Chicago Coliseum, the delegates at the Republican National Convention were ending another sweltering day of political deadlock. Hot and tired, they could not choose a candidate for the upcoming presidential election. As the Republicans left the convention hall on Friday night, June 11, 1920, they were eager for both a break in the weather and in the voting stalemate.

Most of the delegates stayed up throughout the long hot night, meeting in small, private groups in the rooms of the Blackstone Hotel. They talked about how to end the standstill so they could wind up the convention and go home.

A PERSISTENT CANDIDATE

General Leonard Wood and Frank O. Lowden, the governor of Illinois, were the clear front-runners in the race. Senator Hiram Johnson of California had also been a leader in the primary elections in his state. They were followed by several other candidates, jostling each other for position and delegate support.

Among the many contestants for the Republican presidential nomination was Senator Warren G. Harding of Ohio. In April, Harding had won only a few delegates in the Ohio and Indiana primaries. He had been greatly discouraged in his quest for the nomination, particularly by the weak support in his home state. After the primaries, *The New York Times* considered Harding's campaign a lost cause. "Harding is eliminated. Even if his name is presented to the convention . . . everyone will know that he is an impossible candidate."

Nevertheless, Harding persisted, and his name was included in the list of Republican hopefuls. By late Friday night, June 11, it had become clear that neither Wood nor Lowden had enough support to capture the nomination. To win, a candidate needed 493 delegate votes. Wood led on the first ballot with 287½ votes. Lowden received 211½ votes; Johnson, 133½; and Harding struggled behind with only 65½ votes.

By the fourth ballot, Wood had 314½ votes and Lowden 289. Johnson had come to the convention with 112 committed delegates, but after the first roll call he began to lose votes, and most considered him out of the race. Harding barely hung on with 61½ votes.

Moving Up

At this point, the convention chairman, Senator Henry Cabot Lodge of Massachusetts, called for an adjournment. The battle between Wood and Lowden promised to be a long, bitter fight. Party leaders would not allow it to continue. With the delegates splintering off in all directions on such an important question, it looked as if the Republicans could not find a presidential candidate they were truly enthusiastic about. They needed one candidate to emerge from the pack with strong support, or the American voter would not have confidence in their choice.

With a bang of Lodge's gavel, the convention was adjourned until Saturday morning. At the time, Senator Smoot of Utah was asked why some party leaders, like Lodge, insisted on adjournment. Smoot replied, "Oh, there's going to be a deadlock and we'll have to work out some solution; we wanted the night to think it over." At least the delegates had a chance to leave the convention floor—the temperature had risen to 106 degrees!

At 10 A.M. the next morning, the stuffy, crowded hall was filled again with delegates and onlookers as the convention reconvened. Lodge brought the group to order, and the roll call for the fifth ballot was begun. There was not much difference in the voting than the night before. Wood's support fell to 299 votes and Lowden was now ahead with 303. Johnson continued to lose ground while Harding moved up with 78 votes. Despite the long, hot night of political wheeling and dealing, the deadlock and disharmony continued.

Gaining Momentum

By the seventh ballot, however, there was a distinct shift in delegate support. Harding was the only candidate to gain a large number of votes. With 16 new votes, his total increased to 105. The leaders, Wood and Lowden, remained in the same stalemated position, while Johnson fell back behind Harding. On the eighth ballot, the trend became even stronger. Harding gained another 28½ votes. Rumors spread on the convention floor that support for the Ohio senator was snowballing, and he would soon be the winner.

Chairman Lodge stepped in again, this time calling for a recess in the proceedings. This was a bad break for Harding, who was on the verge of causing a stampede of delegates to break ranks and fall in behind him. Timing was crucial. A recess might cause his supporters to lose momentum, and Harding was still far short of the votes he needed to win.

During the recess, Wood and Lowden conferred. They both realized that they were about to see the nomination swept away by Harding. Yet they could not compromise and join forces. Neither would agree to take second place on the other's ticket. Both demanded top billing as President.

The recess dragged on. Finally, Lowden decided to release his delegates to Harding. He could see that he had lost his bid for the presidency, and he believed that Harding was closer to his own position on most issues than was Wood. Some of his delegates had already gone over to Harding's camp. If the rest deserted him for Harding, he would simply be humiliated by their defection. Months before, Harding had been wise enough to establish a more or less friendly relationship with Lowden. Knowing that Harding rarely forgot a friend or a favor, Lowden calculated that he now had more to gain by willingly throwing his support to Harding.

After the recess ended, the ninth ballot was begun. It very quickly became apparent that a move to nominate Harding was sweeping across the convention floor like wildfire.

Connecticut's 14 votes had been Lowden's. But on the ninth ballot the hoarse delegates from the Nutmeg State shouted out that all but one were now voting for Harding. Florida and Kansas, which had both supported Wood, now switched over to Harding, too. Soon after the Harding bandwagon gained all 26 of Kansas' votes, 12 more came from Louisiana, 36 from Missouri, and a whopping 66 from New York.

At the end of the roll call, Harding was the clear leader with 374 votes. Wood had 249, and Lowden, who had released most of his delegates to Harding, had 121½. The convention floor was in an uproar. Harding supporters demonstrated in the aisles, marching with banners and signs. They called out to other delegates to climb on the bandwagon and come along with the winner. Chairman Lodge banged his gavel, calling for order. But the convention floor was caught in a feverish swell of excitement and beyond control.

An Accidental Stabbing

During the balloting, Harry Daugherty, Harding's campaign manager, rushed up to the balcony to join Mrs. Harding. The hall was hot and airless, and the events of the past few hours had been so trying that Daugherty feared Mrs. Harding might be about to faint.

Mrs. Harding had not wanted her husband to run for President. But since he had come this far, she urged him to stick it out. On Friday she had told the press, "I cannot see why anyone should want to be President. . . . I can see but one word written over the head of my husband if he is elected, and that word is 'Tragedy.' "

Mrs. Harding was referring to her husband's weak heart and the health problems that had plagued him for years. She had seen President Wilson's health worn away by the duties of his office and was afraid that the same thing would happen to her husband. Unfortunately, her pessimistic vision eventually proved true.

When Daugherty joined her in the balcony as the ninth ballot was being called, Mrs. Harding was pale and overwhelmed by the excitement. She sat clutching her hat in one hand and her long hat pins (which were fashionable at the time) in the other. Daugherty explained that it looked like her husband would win the nomination on the next ballot.

Mrs. Harding was so shocked she leaped up from her chair. Hoping to catch her if she fell, Daugherty jumped up too, and Mrs. Harding accidentally stabbed him with her hatpins. At the time, he wanted to scream from the pain, but, without saying a word, he waited until Mrs. Harding was calmer. Then Daugherty returned to the floor, feeling dizzy himself. He was sure that the hat pins had pierced his lungs, and that he was about to faint from a loss of blood without seeing Harding's momentous and unexpected triumph. As it turned out, the hatpins had barely scratched him. Daugherty was only excited – almost as overwhelmed as Mrs. Harding.

VICTORY AT LAST

On the 10th ballot, Harding had 440 votes by the time the roll call reached Pennsylvania. Only 53 more were needed to win the nomination. When Pennsylvania gave Harding 61 votes, the race was over. A deafening cheer filled the hall. Lowden, Wood, and others could no longer deny their defeat. After the balloting ended with 692½ votes for Harding, the nomination was quickly declared unanimous.

In the same wild, chaotic swell of excitement, the delegates quickly chose a candidate for Vice-President. Some party leaders had wanted to nominate a Senator Lenroot to run with Harding. But someone stood up on a chair and yelled out, "Calvin Coolidge!" The name of the conservative governor of Massachusetts immediately appealed to the crowd. Coolidge had recently attracted national attention by his actions during the Boston police strike. "There is no right to strike against the public safety by anybody, anytime, anywhere," Coolidge told the policemen's union. His antilabor stand presented an image of a strong, decisive statesman and the delegates quickly added Coolidge to the Harding ticket.

After the convention was officially adjourned, the delegates quickly rushed from the stuffy hall. Little did they realize they had not only chosen the 29th President of the United States, they had also picked his successor.

Chapter 2

The Boy from Blooming Grove

When Warren G. Harding was born on November 2, 1865, his mother took great care in choosing his middle name. She finally settled on "Gamaliel," a name from the Old Testament which she hoped would mark her firstborn to be a minister and a teacher. Her expectations for her eldest child were certainly far more modest than the office of President of the United States. But Phoebe Dickerson Harding always believed that her son was destined to distinguish himself, and she tried to prepare him for high achievement as best as she could.

Warren was a beautiful baby, so "pretty," in fact, that he was sometimes mistaken for a girl. The Hardings had eight children altogether, but Warren always remained a particular favorite of his mother. Two of his younger siblings died in childhood.

The family first lived in a small frame farmhouse just outside of Blooming Grove, a village in northern Ohio. The modest, two-story house had a porch in front, a few shade trees, and a well in the side yard. It was built on a knoll that overlooked rolling, lush farmland. Harding's great-great grandfather had come to Ohio from Pennsylvania and had cleared a small homestead for his family. The land passed from father to son and finally to George Tyron Harding, Warren's father.

A SECRET MARRIAGE

Before George Tyron Harding had any ideas about marriage and children, he yearned to serve in the Civil War. Short and slim, he was not very strong, but he managed to pass the Army physical. However, before he saw any fighting, he became sick, was hospitalized, and then discharged.

One night after George had returned home from the Army, he and Phoebe Dickerson met at a skating party. They had grown up together and had always liked each other. That night, they held hands under the blankets of a horse-drawn sleigh. A month later, George and Phoebe were secretly engaged.

But before settling down to married life, George still wanted to take part in the Civil War. As soon as he was well enough, he re-enlisted in the Army, this time to serve as a drummer. The day before his departure from Blooming Grove, he and Phoebe decided to elope. They were married by a minister in a nearby town with Phoebe's sister as their only witness.

Because George was not yet 21, he needed a note from his father giving permission for him to get married. But the couple decided to keep their marriage a secret until after George returned from the war, and they persuaded his father and Phoebe's sister not to tell anyone. The secret was so well kept, in fact, that while in the Army, George was stationed with another young man from Blooming Grove who liked Phoebe and wrote to her often. He even showed George the brief, friendly letter Phoebe wrote back. George's friend had

George Tyron Harding, Warren's father, built a house for his family on the same site his grandparents had built their first log cabin when they settled in Ohio. (Library of Congress.)

no idea he was actually writing to Mrs. George Tyron Harding!

Becoming a Doctor

Once again, George became ill while in the Army and needed to be hospitalized. When the news reached Blooming Grove, Phoebe's parents could not understand why she was so upset. When she insisted on going to Cleveland to nurse George, the truth about their secret marriage was revealed. Although Phoebe's father did not favor the match, he did not attempt to keep the couple apart.

When George and Phoebe returned to Blooming Grove, they lived for a time with his family. Then George built a small house on the Harding land, on the same site where his grandparents had built their first log cabin when they settled in Ohio. It was about this time that their son, Warren Gamaliel, was born.

George taught in a nearby one-room schoolhouse for a short time but soon became bored with the profession. He then earned a living by doing some farming and by working as a self-taught veterinarian. A few years after Warren was born, George bought a secondhand set of medical books and began to read about medicine. He accompanied a country doctor on his rounds, spent two terms at the Western College of Homeopathy in Cleveland, and received his medical degree in 1873.

In the hopes of building up his practice, Dr. Harding moved the family from the Blooming Grove homestead to the outskirts of Caledonia and later to Marion, a larger town about 25 miles away. But Dr. Harding was never very successful. Phoebe, who served as a midwife delivering babies, often had more patients than her husband.

The Hardings' Special Talent

Some accounts describe Dr. Harding as lazy, impractical, and a daydreamer. It is said he was more interested in making a good trade or "swap" than he was in medicine. Dr. Harding was known to "swap" with anyone, anytime, for just about anything. Trading livestock, farm machinery or tools, land, or just the use of land for planting or grazing, was a common practice at that time for farmers, who were generally short of cash.

With eight children to provide for, Dr. Harding was always struggling to make ends meet. Trading something the family did not need for something it did was an important talent that supplemented his faltering medical practice. Warren Harding was later to be known as an expert negotiator, able to bring almost any two disagreeing parties together and help them work out some kind of compromise—a talent he most likely learned from his father.

A Mother's Lasting Influence

Warren Harding grew up in a strict Christian household. His father was a Baptist, and his mother was a devout Methodist who attended church daily. She also took the family to Sunday services and church suppers. Phoebe was a hardworking and seemingly tireless woman. She often quoted Scripture and hummed hymns as she cared for her eight children, cooked, baked, sewed, and kept an orderly household. Despite the many demands of her large family, she also found time to work as a midwife.

Warren Harding's mother, from whom he inherited his dark eyes and calm, gentle expression, was a great influence on him. Before he was four years old, she had taught him the alphabet. Because the family did not have a blackboard or chalk, they wrote with a stick of charred wood on the bottom of a shoebox. His mother also gave Warren his first reading lessons from pages in the Bible and from a copy of the local newspaper, the *Marion County Sentinel,* which she pasted on the woodbox next to the stove. And she taught him to memorize poems and recite them to company. When the Hardings went visiting, Warren would always be eager to "deliver his piece."

Even as Warren grew older, his mother remained an important influence in his life. Every Sunday morning he would bring her flowers or make sure that they were delivered to her by a florist. In the White House, he kept her photograph on his desk. Phoebe Harding had great love for her son and was confident that he would do well at whatever he tried.

Warren Harding was the oldest of eight children. Seen here seated between his sister Charity (left) and Mary (right), he was about nine years old. (Library of Congress.)

SCHOOL DAYS

Harding's family and friends gave him the nickname "Winnie." Growing up in the Ohio countryside, he enjoyed the pastimes most other boys did — swimming, fishing, and playing baseball. He was a hard worker, especially when there was a chance to earn some money. At 10 years old, he had his first paying job cutting corn. By 14, he was helping out at nearby farms by painting barns, milking cows, currying (grooming) horses, and thrashing grain.

Warren began his education at a one-room schoolhouse in Blooming Grove. When the family moved to Caledonia, he gained a reputation in his new school for his ability to spell long words and to speak before a group. He was not a particularly hardworking student, but most teachers considered him smarter than his classmates.

Warren never stood out as a leader in school; he seemed more content just to be one of the gang. He impressed most people as a boy who was kind to others, had a good sense of humor, was friendly, and was easy to get along with.

One day when Warren was about 10 years old, his father came home with a B-flat cornet he had picked up in a trade. A local harness maker gave Warren music lessons, and in a short time he played well enough to join the Caledonia Aeolian Band. The band performed every Saturday night on the bandstand in town and sometimes traveled to other towns nearby. Warren greatly enjoyed playing the cornet in the group, and one of his boyhood friends later said that "barring the bass drummer, no other member of the band could make as much noise."

At about the same time that Harding's father brought home the cornet, he made another trade and became the owner of a local newspaper, the *Caledonia Argus*. The *Argus* was a struggling operation that had no regular publication schedule. The previous owner, Will Warner, would print the *Argus* whenever he could afford to buy some paper.

A Printer's Devil

At the offices of the *Argus,* Warren had his first sniff of printer's ink and his first taste of newspaper work. He would never get the love of newspaper work out of his blood. Even as President, he would sometimes daydream about the time he could leave Washington and become a newspaper editor again.

When Dr. Harding took over the paper, Will Warner agreed to stay on and run it. Warner was a bit eccentric and wore a top hat constantly. He had run the paper as a one-man operation, performing as publisher, editor, reporter, type-setter, advertising salesman, and circulation manager, not to mention office janitor. After ownership changed hands, Warren went to work there. He became an office errand boy, or apprentice printer, commonly known as a "printer's devil."

From Warner, Warren Harding learned all there was to know about running a newspaper. He did the hard, dirty jobs like sweeping floors, delivering papers, and washing down the press. Will Warner eventually taught Warren how to set type and run the press.

A Good Luck Charm

One night, Warner needed help on a special "rush" print job. The inexperienced Warren Harding was the only person around who could help him. After working hard together all night long, Will Warner thought the boy deserved a special gift.

The next day Will gave Warren a tool that only profes-sional typesetters used. It was a steel ruler called a make-up rule. Although it was not an expensive present, it did show that Warren had earned Will's respect. Harding held onto the make-up rule for his entire life and considered it his good luck charm.

In addition to teaching Warren the nuts and bolts of putting out a newspaper, Will Warner also taught him the values that a small-town publisher needed. These values, which included civic pride, promoting local business, being a good neighbor, having an optimistic attitude, and making a contribution to the community, made a lasting impression on Warren.

COLLEGE DAYS

When Warren was 14, he went off to study at Ohio Central College in nearby Iberia. Like most of the students at the college, Warren planned to become a teacher. Starting college at 14 was not uncommon at the time. However, pursuing a college education was, especially for an Ohio boy from a modest background.

Ohio Central had a very small faculty by today's standards – only two clergymen and a professor of ancient languages – and the curriculum was somewhat meager. Warren studied arithmetic, history, grammar, and some science, but he was not a very dedicated student. He was far more interested in making friends, debating, and editing the school newspaper, the *Iberian Spectator.*

Warren started the paper himself with the help of a friend. It had four pages, the usual size for a country paper at that time, and was quite popular. It included local news, advertisements, jokes, and an editorial. Warren once wrote in an editorial that families who did not subscribe to the paper were "stingy old grumblers" who "take no more interest in home enterprise than a mule does a hive of bees." The paper only lasted six issues but marked the highlight of his college days.

SOME STARTS AND STOPS

Warren graduated from Ohio Central College in 1882, when he was 17 years old. His graduating class was small, only two other students and himself. Always known as a good public speaker, he was chosen to deliver the commencement address.

After graduation, Warren returned home to Marion, where the family now lived. He took a position teaching in a schoolhouse north of town. But in just a few months, he realized that, despite his mother's wish for him, he was not cut out for the life of a rural schoolteacher. In a letter to his aunt at the end of the school year, he wrote, "I believe my calling to be in some other sphere and will follow out that belief."

After teaching for a year, Warren tried a few other professions, but without much success. He became an insurance salesman but quit after frequently making mistakes figuring out policy rates. Dr. Harding picked up some law books in a trade, and Warren read law for awhile. But despite his talent for speaking and debating, the study of law did not hold his interest for long.

Back to the Presses

Newspaper ink had gotten into Warren's blood, and once again he was lured back to the presses, the only work he really liked. His father arranged for Warren to take a job on the *Mirror,* a newspaper in Marion. Colonel James Vaughan ran the paper, and Warren was hired as an all-around hand — reporter, advertising salesman, and delivery boy.

Vaughan fired Warren after only a brief time, however, reportedly because he was spending too much time loafing with his friends in town. Warren already had a reputation in town for idling away an afternoon, exchanging stories and gossip, and discussing politics. He even had a name for his favorite pastime —"bloviating." Vaughan, who was a Democrat, perhaps would not have minded Warren's "bloviating" so much if the young man had not been practicing his talent with Republicans at the local party headquarters. However, whatever their political differences, Harding and Vaughan parted on good terms.

As in his break with Vaughan, Warren rarely made enemies. Somehow, the charming, people-pleasing young man always managed to remain friendly, even with those with whom he had differences. All through his life, this personality characteristic served him well, particularly once he began his political career.

Opportunity Knocks

Getting fired from the *Mirror* had been discouraging for Warren, but it hardly soured his love for newspaper work. A short time later, he and two of his friends decided to get together and buy the Marion *Star.* The *Star* was a five-column, four-page newspaper that was struggling along with a subscription list of little over 500.

Warren's partners, Jack Warwick and Johnnie Sickle, were old friends and both former members of the Caledonia Aeolian Band. Each of the three put up $100 to buy the paper. Sickle had recently inherited some money, so he supplied both his share and Warwick's.

Warren did not have the money. However, instead of borrowing it from Sickle, as Warwick had done, he asked his former boss, Colonel Vaughan, for a loan. He cleverly convinced the colonel to help him by pointing out that the *Star* was a Republican paper and it would be keen competition for the colonel's only rival, the Republican *Independent.*

His apprenticeship with Will Warner now served Warren well. The three partners did everything—the writing, editing, typesetting, selling ads and subscriptions, bookkeeping, and delivering. In 1884 the population of Marion was only 4,000. Yet three newspapers—each with only a few pages of print—managed to survive because of political connections.

A Winning Editorial Policy

Already politically minded, Warren could see he had a chance with the *Star.* Even though the county was largely Democratic, the town itself and the state were controlled by Republicans. He employed a successful nonpartisan editorial policy of praising the Republicans but never damning the Democrats.

With this policy, Warren not only avoided making enemies among the Democratic advertisers, he also won them away from the *Independent,* eventually putting his rival out of business altogether. Under Harding's direction, the *Star* became even more influential than Vaughan's Democratic *Mirror,* which must have given Warren some private satisfaction when he recalled how the colonel had once fired him.

Every morning, Warren would walk to his office in the center of town from his family's home in a poor section of Marion. He was a dignified figure, but always friendly and relaxed. Everyone in town knew him, and he always had time to stop and chat, to inquire about business or family, or to trade an interesting tidbit of gossip.

Working with "W.G."

Harding was known fondly in the newspaper office as W.G. Even after the paper prospered and the staff grew, he liked to hang around with his employees in the newsroom or pressroom and share a plug of chewing tobacco. He took a paternal interest in the newsboys and vagrant tramp printers who would drift in and out of the press room. He allowed these homeless men to sleep in the newspaper offices. He liked his office so much that he often slept there himself.

Harding was an easygoing boss and was well liked by his employees. Reportedly, he never raised his voice or lost his temper. He treated the staff of the *Star* as a family and rarely fired anyone. Yet, the good-natured boss was ambitious and had plans for his future. He wanted to acquire complete control of the paper, and eventually he did.

When Sickle decided to move West, Warren bought his share. Later, Warwick lost his share of the *Star* to Harding in a poker game. As was Harding's way, he and Warwick remained good friends. Warwick continued to work at the *Star,* eventually as managing editor. He once praised Harding's democratic attitude toward his employees by saying, "He was one of us and he insisted that we worked 'with him' not 'for him.' "

Harding's attitude towards his employees at the *Star* reflected his belief in what he termed the "democracy" of small town life. In later political speeches, Harding would define this philosophy, saying:

> I do not believe that anywhere in the world there is so perfect a democracy as in the village. . . . There is no social strata or society requirement in the village. About everybody starts equal . . . the blacksmith's son and the cobbler's son and the minister's son and the storekeeper's son all had just the same chance in the opportunities of this America as ours.

Harding was perhaps an ideal example of his belief. Starting with very little, he had worked hard, been resourceful, and was even daring. Most people thought of him as easygoing and not particularly competitive. He had a charitable streak and often lent a helping hand to those who were worse off than himself. But Harding always made the most of any opportunity that came his way. By his early twenties, he owned a successful business and was a well-liked and respected figure in Marion—the very image of a self-made man.

THE ELIGIBLE BACHELOR AND "THE DUCHESS"

From being attractive as a child, Warren Harding grew into a strikingly handsome young man. His good looks, business success, and natural talent for putting people at ease made him one of the town's most eligible bachelors.

Surprising many in Marion, Warren married Florence Kling De Wolfe on July 8 in 1891. It was about seven years after he had taken over the *Star;* he was almost 26 years old. Flossie, as she was known to family and friends, was 31 and divorced.

Flossie's father, Amos Kling, was known to be tyrannical and ambitious. Starting out with a modest hardware business, Kling then moved his financial interests into real estate. About the time Warren and Flossie were married, her father had financed the construction of the recently built Marion Hotel at a cost of $30,000, which made him the wealthiest man in Marion.

Flossie Kling had obviously inherited her father's strong will and determination. It is said that she set her sights on Warren and pursued him openly, despite the fact that her father was violently opposed to the marriage. This was no great obstacle to Flossie, who had already married once against family wishes when she eloped at 19 with Henry A. (Peter) De Wolfe.

Pete De Wolfe was the flashy, spoiled son of a distinguished Marion family. An alcoholic, he abandoned Flossie and their year-old son, Marshall. After his parents' divorce, the boy was largely ignored by Flossie and raised by his Kling grandparents.

After her divorce, Florence was not welcomed to live in her father's home. She had studied music and earned her living giving piano lessons. She and Warren first met in the front parlor of his family's home while Florence was giving a piano lesson to his younger sister, Chat.

A Decisive, Purposeful Woman

Flossie Kling and Warren Harding seemed an unlikely match to many. Flossie was not an exceptionally attractive woman, either physically or in her manner. She was plain-featured, somewhat ungainly, known to have a sharp tongue, and was sometimes haughty in manner. In many ways, she was the very opposite of Warren, who was both good looking and went out of his way to get along with almost everyone he met. Flossie's bright blue eyes were her loveliest feature, reflecting a decisive, purposeful mind.

It was perhaps those qualities that attracted Harding to her. Much like his mother, Flossie had an unshakable loyalty to "her Warren" and a firm faith that he would eventually rise to great achievements. Harding perhaps recognized in himself some of his father's traits for idleness and daydreaming. But taking a wife like Flossie was insurance against backsliding and the tendency towards too much "bloviating." Throughout their lifetime together, Harding called Flossie "the Duchess," a nickname that characterized her regal demeanor and sense of high standards.

Amos Kling did not approve of the editor of the Marion *Star*. Once he and Harding met by chance in the local courthouse and the two nearly came to blows. Kling did not attend his daughter's wedding, and it was 14 years later before he allowed Flossie to enter his home.

After their marriage, the couple moved into a new house that Warren had built at 380 Mount Vernon Avenue. Throughout that year, he suffered fits of indigestion, a health problem he would never fully overcome. At the end of the year, he visited a health sanitarium at Battle Creek, Michigan, for two months. It was run by a well-known vegetarian physician, Dr. John Kellogg (who later became famous for his corn flakes). Harding returned home to Marion, but when he was overcome again by the painful, chronic ailment, he returned to Battle Creek for another five-month stay.

A Perfect Partnership

From the start of their marriage, Florence Harding became very active in the newspaper business. As she later explained, she went down to the office to lend a hand temporarily and the arrangement lasted "for fourteen years." Flossie had a keen mind for business and a talent for managing the departments her husband found boring. She set up a carrier delivery system and introduced an improved bookkeeping system.

Harding was free to devote himself to those areas he most enjoyed: editorial matters, selling advertising, and public relations. Because he sold advertising space in the paper himself, he became acquainted with all the businessmen in town.

Despite the rumors in Marion, Florence Harding was not the "power behind the throne" at the *Star,* and not the sole reason for the paper's ever-increasing influence. Florence never intruded into the policy of the paper, did any reporting, or wrote editorials. Her contributions were limited to office management. Her husband later praised her as "a good businesswoman," but to many on the staff, Mrs. Harding did appear to "run the show."

Some said that Warren found it convenient to have people believe that his wife controlled the newspaper. He never liked to refuse anyone a favor or request. If employees wanted a raise, "W.G." could always use the excuse that he would have been willing, but his wife refused. But behind the scenes, he still had the last word on all major financial decisions.

Whatever his expectations were at the time of their marriage, Harding had to have been pleased by the productive business partnership he and his wife shared. Flossie's contributions to the *Star* were important to the growth of the paper and perhaps crucial to the success of Warren's political aspirations. While "the Duchess" managed the office, he was able to set the groundwork for his political career.

Marion's Leading "Booster"

During his years as Marion's leading newspaper publisher, Harding belonged to just about every civic and philanthropic organization in town. He was a member of the Elks, the Rotary, and a respectable (although not particularly religious) attendant of the Baptist church. He served as chairman of all the important committees of the Marion Chamber of Commerce and also became a director of the Marion County Bank. He sat on the board of the local telephone company and the building and loan association, as well as the Marion Lumber Company. And—if all this activity was not enough of a display of his civic spirit—he continued to play his B-flat cornet in the marching band.

Also known as a great city "booster," Harding was always willing to help new businesses get off the ground by buying shares. Sometimes these shares proved to be worthless investments. But Harding was not interested only in a financial return. He was, in a sense, investing in his own reputation as a civic leader and promoting himself. He was already involved in politics on a local level.

Chapter 3
The Great Harmonizer

When Harding took over the *Star* in 1884, the surrounding fields around Marion were abundant with alfalfa and corn. The small, sleepy village of 4,000 people had once been a market town and then a grain center. With the coming of the railroad, industry sprang up as well.

Marion grew and the circulation of Harding's newspaper grew with it. By 1890 there were 8,000 people in Marion; by 1900, nearly 12,000; and by 1910, 18,000. New neighborhoods with fine new homes were going up in all directions as the town's limits expanded outward. The Harding home was one of these, with a broad front porch, columns and railings, and a wide green lawn. New businesses and stores lined the main street. There was plenty of new enterprise for the Marion *Star* to applaud — the groundbreaking for a new church, a new music hall, a new school.

Even before buying the *Star*, Harding had always had a strong interest in politics. As a young man, he had attended county caucuses (meetings to choose candidates for office) and large political meetings. His father was a Republican, and after buying the *Star*, Warren also supported Republican doctrines. As the newspaper grew, so did Harding's influence in political circles.

The Hardings' home on Mount Vernon Avenue in Marion, Ohio, was dark green with white trim. Its wide porch was purposely rebuilt as a stage for campaign speeches. (Library of Congress.)

STATE SENATOR

In 1887, at the age of 22, Harding went to his first state convention as the Republican delegate of Marion County. This convention was the first of many that would follow. In 1895, he was asked to run for county auditor, although there was no chance that a Republican could win. Nevertheless, Harding ran and took the loss in his typical obliging manner, thereby proving his party loyalty.

In 1898 Harding ran for the Ohio Senate and won. He had a reputation for honesty in an era and political structure that tolerated graft (gain through dishonest means). Yet he was not out to make waves for those who did not share his standards of virtue. On legislative issues as well, he generally stuck to the middle course and had a talent for winning the goodwill of those on both sides of the question.

The positions Harding was to bring to the White House on many issues were already emerging. In regard to tariffs (taxes on imported goods), he was protectionist, believing that high duties increased workers' wages and protected the American standard of living. He was suspicious of immigration, especially the new wave of immigrants from southern and eastern Europe. He distrusted labor unions, although he was not adamant on the subject. He wavered on the prohibition of alcohol issue. Harding was not "dry" himself, but he did recognize that the supporters of prohibition were strong in Ohio. He voted on this issue in whatever direction the political wind seemed to blow at the time.

Getting Things Done

"There may be an abler man in the Senate than Harding," Ohio's governor once said, "but when I want things done, I go to him." Because of his talent as a conciliator between political factions, Harding was known for getting results.

Early in his political career, the new state senator's approach to disagreement was an attitude of compromise and harmony. It proved a powerful political tool in Harding's hands. One observer at the time said, "In the Ohio Senate, Harding proved a great harmonizer. He had the unusual gift of getting people together and inducing them to patch up differences."

Harding served two terms in the State Senate, four years

altogether. In 1902 he ran for lieutenant governor on Myron T. Herrick's ticket and won. For the next two years, he presided as mediator over the State Senate, a position that broadened his contacts and influence.

It was widely known that Herrick could not win a second term, and Harding had his eye on the office of governor himself. But his ambitions were blocked when Herrick decided to run again. Harding did not have enough backing in his party to oppose Herrick. Despite his ambitions, it was important for him to give way as gracefully as he could, and to adhere to his own policy of harmony for the greater good of the party.

Back to Marion

After his term as lieutenant governor ended in 1905, Harding took a break from politics and returned to Marion. It had been extremely difficult for him to run the newspaper from the state capital of Columbus. Also, at about this time, Flossie Harding had become seriously ill with a kidney ailment and needed more of his attention. Warren felt he had gone far enough in his political career for now; it was time to attend to his personal and business affairs.

Harding did not leave Columbus with any regrets. His tenure in the state capital had been successful, and he had built up a strong base of goodwill and important contacts. He knew that sometime in the future he would have the necessary support to run for governor or a seat in the United States Senate.

Returning to his editorship of the *Star,* Harding remained close to political circles. He continued to play the role of harmonizer for warring political factions, and he stayed in the mainstream of political trends, often helping to shape popular opinion himself through his *Star* editorials.

An Unfaithful Husband

Reportedly, Harding was frequently unfaithful to his wife. One of the longest and best documented of his relationships with other women involved Carrie Phillips. She was the wife of James E. Phillips, a part owner of the Uhler-Phillips dry goods store in Harding's hometown of Marion, Ohio.

Neighbors and friends, the Hardings and Phillipses socialized frequently. A former school teacher, Carrie was by all accounts strikingly attractive, one of the most beautiful women in Marion. Nine years younger than Harding, she was also intelligent, charming, and considerably more sophisticated than others in their social circle.

The relationship between Carrie and Harding began in the spring of 1905 and lasted for 15 years, until the time of his presidential campaign in 1920. During the intervening years, there were several breakups and reconciliations. Carrie did not encourage Harding to pursue his political ambitions, perhaps because she considered his political aspirations a threat to their relationship and the future they could presumably have if Harding were to leave his wife. At that time, divorce was rare but not unheard of. (Even Florence Harding had been divorced from her first husband before marrying Warren.) However, because divorce was certainly unacceptable for a politician who aspired toward high office, the relationship between Carrie and Harding ended after he was nominated for the presidency in 1920.

RUNNING FOR GOVERNOR

In 1910 Harding decided it was time to go back into politics. Judson Harmon, a Democrat, had been elected governor of Ohio in 1908 and was now running for a second term. Warren's friends encouraged him to run against Harmon, but he was a bit reluctant. Although he wanted to be governor, he was not sure he could win the election or even the nomination of his party.

A tireless writer of notes and letters, Harding had been careful to stay in touch with acquaintances throughout the state who would support him—businessmen, politicians, and fellow newspaper owners. Now he decided to take a chance and run. At the Republican State Convention, he won the nomination.

However, even at this point it seemed that Harding knew the odds were against him beating Harmon. Early in the race, Warren was reported to have said that he would have given a thousand dollars to have *lost* his party's nomination. The problem was that many progressive Republicans liked the Democratic Governor Judson Harmon better than their own candidate, Harding. Although Harding, the Great Harmonizer, tried to unite his party's support behind him, the progressive faction still considered him too conservative and "middle of the road" for their liking.

A Discouraging Loss

Harding lost the election for governor by 100,000 votes, and the Democrats won 16 of 21 seats in Congress. It was the most important defeat in his political career and served as a discouraging lesson about the unpredictable ups and downs of a life in politics.

Before the election, Harding had written to his sister, "This time I shall attain the very distinguished honor or I shall henceforth and forever free myself from all public political participation—and be much better off."

After his defeat, Harding expressed the same sentiments in a letter to a fellow newspaper owner who had encouraged

him to run. He claimed he felt calm and settled in his decision to drop out of politics – this time, forever. He was glad
to be rid of the goading political bug that had urged him on,
only to be disappointed, and he was free of the constant worry
of having to explain where he stood on the isssues. He was
eager to pursue other interests that would prove more
satisfying.

PRESIDENT TAFT'S INVITATION

It seemed to many close to Harding that his decision to re-
tire from politics was final this time. But in 1912 he was lured
back into the political arena by a special request from President William Howard Taft. In 1908, when Taft was seeking
the Republican nomination for President, Harding had taken
a risky political step by leaving his old allies, who supported
other candidates, and giving his support to the Taft ticket.
Taft won the nomination and was elected President.

When Taft decided to run for a second term, he asked
Warren to place his name in nomination at the Republican
National Convention in 1912. Harding was greatly honored
by Taft's invitation. It was not only a tribute to his ability as
a speaker, but also to his reputation as a party figure who
could bring harmony to the convention. Two conflicting
groups were now trying to gain control of the party. A faction known as the Progressives wanted the convention to nominate Theodore Roosevelt, who had already served two terms
as President from 1901 to 1908. The "regular" or more conservative Republicans supported Taft's re-election.

It was normal for an incumbent President (a President
presently in office) to be supported by his party. It was up
to Harding to bring these warring groups together with his
nominating speech. He knew the task would not be easy. He

hoped to convince the Progressives that Taft shared their views. For the sake of party loyalty, he urged, all Republicans should fall behind President Taft.

Attacking Roosevelt and the Progressives

When Harding began his speech to nominate Taft, his soothing words were hissed, booed, and heckled by Roosevelt supporters. Shocked, he reacted angrily to the agitators. It was one of the few times Harding was ever known to lose his temper in public.

Putting his notes aside, Harding attacked Roosevelt and his supporters, saying their opposition to Taft's renomination was disloyal and without cause or "conscience." He claimed Roosevelt inspired support with "pap rather than patriotism."

The convention floor was in an uproar; delegates were walking out, others were fighting in the aisles. Harding returned to his planned words, which calmly praised Taft and called for party unity. When the vote was called, the delegates who supported Roosevelt sat silent and still. They refused to vote and claimed the convention was a sham, a "railroading" of Roosevelt. Taft was eventually officially nominated by the mainstream delegates.

Harding's nominating speech did not bring the results he had hoped for. But few had expected the progressive element of the party to be so uncompromising. Roosevelt and his supporters could not tolerate Taft's nomination. They marched out of the Republican Party and became the new Progressive Party, also called the Bull Moose Party. (The expression had been coined when reporters asked Roosevelt how he felt and he replied, "As fit as a Bull Moose.") At a convention in August, they named their own candidate, Theodore Roosevelt, for President.

During the campaign months, Harding fought the

Progressives in the *Star,* calling Roosevelt ambitious, ruthless, and "the greatest fakir [imposter] of all times." In November, both Roosevelt and Taft lost the election to the Democratic candidate, Woodrow Wilson.

When Harding returned to Marion after the Republican National Convention, it soon became clear that his appearance at the convention was going to have some important effects on his own political career. For one thing, for the first time, Americans all over the country were now aware of the name Warren G. Harding. Also, in regard to Ohio politics, he had shown himself to be loyal to the conservative, mainstream faction of his party. There was soon talk that Harding would make an excellent candidate for the United States Senate in 1914.

ON TO WASHINGTON

The Democrats and Progressives had been very strong in the 1912 election. But by 1914 the tide was again turning towards the mainstream Republicans, both in Ohio and nationally. Wilson was in the White House, and fears of America's involvement in a war in Europe were rising. The Progressives had failed to make Theodore Roosevelt—one of the most popular Americans of his time—President once more. Voters seemed tired of their "reform" ideas.

As the Progressive movement gradually lost steam, many in the new party decided to return to the Republican ranks. When Harding won his party's nomination to run for the U.S. Senate in 1914, his supporters again saw him as a figure who could bring two groups of Republicans together, at least within Ohio. After the state convention, an article in a Cleveland newspaper predicted that Harding would "help draw back to the Republican ranks the few progressives who have not yet decided to return."

In 1914 the Republican Party as a whole did quite well, winning back many of the seats it had lost to the Democrats and Progressives over the last four years. Harding defeated his opponents easily, winning by an impressive 100,000-vote majority. His big victory in the election was of such importance that it would shape his political future. For several reasons, he had now made a giant step into the category of "presidential possibilities."

In Ohio, the Seventeenth Amendment had come into effect. For the first time, U.S. senators were chosen by popular election rather than by the state legislature. Prior to this time, winning a Senate seat was no proof of popular appeal. But now Harding had shown that he had strong public appeal and was successful in bringing in the popular vote. Also, until this time, Harding's political experience had been only within the state of Ohio. As a U.S. senator, he would now take part in the arduous process of solving the problems that faced the entire nation. In Washington, D.C., Warren Gamaliel Harding would be at the very hub of the country's political power and influence.

Chapter 4

The Senate Years

The Hardings were excited about the prospect of living in Washington for the next six years. They bought a large, two-story house on Wyoming Avenue. It was Georgian style and newly built, with a terrace that separated it from the street. The new house cost almost $50,000, which was expensive for 1914. But Harding could afford it. He still owned the *Star,* and as publisher made an income of $20,000 a year, not counting his other financial interests.

The house in Washington was quite formal in contrast to the rambling, "homey" residence back in Ohio. Although impressive, it was perhaps not as comfortable as their old home, and it would take some getting used to. But it was all part of the Hardings' new life in Washington.

NEW HOME, NEW FRIENDS

The Hardings had been leading citizens of Marion, Ohio, and had certainly enjoyed all the privileges of that social position. In spite of Flossie Harding's kidney ailment and related health problems, the couple had traveled widely, to Europe, Hawaii, and throughout the United States.

But now in the nation's capital, the Hardings felt socially ill at ease. Compared to the sophisticated group in Washington, Marion's leading citizens seemed rather naive and lacking in certain social refinements. Warren Harding had been born with a knack for charming new acquaintances and winning them over. Although he might have felt overwhelmed socially, he was good at hiding his uneasiness.

Harding's lack of sophistication even seemed appealing to some, for he never pretended to be anything but himself. For Flossie, however, fitting into Washington social circles was a bit harder. She lacked her husband's good-natured personality, and her poor health often kept her at home in relative isolation.

Princess Alice

Harding had always enjoyed playing golf and sharing a friendly card game with friends in the evenings. In Washington he continued that pastime. The Hardings were invited to card parties at the home of Nick Longworth, a congressman from Ohio. His wife, Alice, was Teddy Roosevelt's daughter, and in the capital's inner circles, she was known as "Princess Alice."

Although it appeared that she did not hold a grudge about Harding's political difference with her father, Alice Roosevelt Longworth was known to consider the Hardings socially inferior. She invited them frequently to her house but never accepted any invitations to visit their home. When Harding had first come to Washington, Alice told others later she disliked his habit of chewing tobacco and considered him "a slob."

The MacLeans

It was at a Longworth card party that the Hardings first met Ned and Evalyn MacLean. The MacLeans were young, unpredictable, outrageously rich, and quite influential in Washington society. Ned MacLean was the heir to the

Washington Post fortune, and Evalyn's father, an Irish immigrant, had become one of the richest men in America when he discovered a gold mine in Colorado.

The MacLeans liked the Hardings after their first meeting at the Longworths. Evalyn in particular thought Harding was "a stunning man" and disagreed with Alice Longworth's insulting assessment of him. Evalyn also felt sorry for Flossie; it was obvious that the older woman was having some trouble becoming accustomed to life in Washington.

Right after meeting the MacLeans, Flossie became critically ill again. Doctor Sawyer, who had treated the Hardings for years in Marion, was sent for. Flossie believed that only her trusted physician from back home could keep her alive. When Evalyn MacLean heard that Flossie was sick, she visited and kept Flossie company at her bedside. She was most sympathetic and very encouraging.

Under Dr. Sawyer's care, Flossie's health gradually improved, and Evalyn's friendship continued. She sent Flossie Harding flowers and took her on trips while she was convalescing. When Flossie was well enough to socialize, Evalyn helped her fit into Washington's social circles.

THE MIDDLE COURSE

During any presidential administration, there is always a struggle between the Senate and President. The powers of the President are outlined by the Constitution, but the extent and expression of those powers are unique to the man in office.

Some Presidents believe their power to be limited and allow the Senate to rule. Under a strong President who holds to the power of his office, the Senate either buckles under or fights. Woodrow Wilson believed in the powers of the presidency. In his book *Constitutional Government in the United States,* he wrote, "The President is at liberty both in the law and conscience, to be as big a man as he can. His capacity will set the limit." Wilson dominated the Senate, much to the dislike of those senators who believed that the Senate, and not the President, should be the more powerful force in government.

An Undistinguished Performance

When Harding came to Washington in 1915 most of the legislative battles over President Wilson's new domestic program had already been settled. After the United States entered World War I in 1917, Wilson continued to overpower the Senate so completely that it was difficult for a junior senator to make a name for himself. Harding was not involved in any issue that would test his abilities to debate on the Senate floor or prove his leadership qualities until after the war, when the Senate fought Wilson on the League of Nations issue.

The single word to describe Harding's performance in the Senate from 1915 to 1921 might be "undistinguished." As a lower-ranking senator, he was assigned a seat in the back rows and put to work on minor Senate committees that rarely provided a strategic political position or a springboard to power. This did not upset Harding, who was primarily concerned with fitting in and was not out to make waves with the more senior senators.

During this time, Harding sat on committees overseeing claims, coastal defenses, expenditures in the Treasury Department, trespasses on Indian lands, and the sale of meat products. His assignment to the Foreign Relations, Commerce and Territories, and Naval Affairs committees were more important tasks, particularly during the war years.

Legislative Record

Harding's legislative record in the Senate was quite unremarkable. He introduced 134 bills, of which 122 had to do with Ohio. Even in regard to his home state, these bills were for minor causes. For example, he initiated one bill to change the name of a Lake Erie steamer and another to secure a Civil War veteran's back pension.

Nor were the other bills that Harding introduced of great national importance. They addressed such minor issues as celebrating the anniversary of the Pilgrims' landing, authorizing the use of federal tents to relieve the 1920 housing shortage, providing funds for the investigation of influenza and other diseases, amending the McKinley Memorial Birthplace Association Act, and giving discarded Army rifles to camps of the Sons of Veterans Reserve.

Harding's attendence at Senate sessions was poor to average. He missed 43 percent of all roll calls; his absences were timed to avoid voting on bills that were controversial. Rather than make enemies, Harding preferred a middle course rather than taking sides on an issue. For example, on bills that had to do with labor, he voted seven times on the side of labor, 11 times against, and was absent 10 times.

MAKING FRIENDS

Washington did not change Harding into a dynamic crusader for the public good. His style as a statesman was not much different on Capitol Hill from what it had been during his years as a state senator in Columbus, Ohio. Now, however, he was on a much higher level to exercise his greatest abilities, which were to be obliging, good-natured, and well liked by all his colleagues, Republicans and Democrats alike.

Harding made friends with established, influential figures such as Oscar Underwood, a Democrat and Wilson's former floor leader in the House. And one of Harding's many golfing partners was the assistant secretary of the Navy and future President, Franklin Delano Roosevelt. The younger, Democratic Roosevelt considered Harding a good sport and "most agreeable" whether he won or lost. The secretary of war, Newton Baker, remembered Harding quite fondly, writing that the Ohio senator "sought to be helpful in every possible way and refrained from any partisan criticism at a time when partisan feelings were very high."

In the back rows of the Senate, Harding made friends with other junior senators. One was James Wadsworth, Jr., from New York, who admired the tough stand Harding had taken against Theodore Roosevelt in 1912. The two became so close that when they were able to move their desks forward, they continued to sit together. Wadsworth wrote of Harding, "He was essentially an honest man. He disliked sham and was deeply concerned over the influence of demagogues [leaders who use devious means to gain power] in American public life."

At this time, Harding also befriended Albert B. Fall, a senator from New Mexico. It was a relationship that would play a great part in the scandalous aftermath of Harding's presidency. Harding may have well been the "essentially honest man" that Wadsworth characterized. But unfortunately, he was either blind to the questionable integrity of some of his associates, like Fall, or he preferred to overlook their shortcomings.

POSITION ON ISSUES

When Harding did vote, his stand on the issues remained basically conservative. Mainly, he voted with the leadership of his party. It would be unfair and an oversimplification to say that Harding was incapable of judging the issues on his own. However, in most situations, his own views of the issues were in harmony with those of the Republican Party.

Harding was, and had always been, in favor of business. He believed that government intervention and control of business ran against basic principles of the American system of capitalism—a system of "survival of the fittest." He felt that many of the business reforms the Progressives had called for in past years were dangerously close to socialism. He was in favor of higher tariffs (taxes on imported goods) and did not believe that farmers should receive subsidies (financial aid) from the federal government.

Suffrage and Prohibition

At this time, women were fighting for suffrage (the right to vote). Also, there was a growing nationwide movement, known as Prohibition, to prohibit the consumption of liquor. A politician's stand on these two issues was important, particularly because both groups—the suffragists and prohibitionists—claimed that they could vote in a "bloc" to support or oppose a candidate's election for office.

Harding was not personally committed to women's suffrage. To a group of suffragists who visited him in Washington in 1915 he said quite frankly that he was "utterly indifferent" to their cause. However, he eventually supported the movement in response to the Republican Party's approval of the question and the tide of positive public opinion within his home state. In 1920, the 19th Amendment to the Constitution gave women the right to vote. Later, in his own presidential election, Harding was helped by the American woman's newly won voting power.

Women's Suffrage

Demands for equality between men and women have been actively voiced in American and European society for more than two centuries. The principles of equality that inspired the American and French revolutions also formed the basis for the feminist movement. Mary Wollstonecraft, an English author, wrote the first major feminist work, *Vindication of the Rights of Woman,* in 1792 in a reaction to the French "Declaration of the Rights of Man."

However, the right to vote, or suffrage, was not the primary issue of the feminist movement in the United States and worldwide. During the 19th century, the feminist movement pushed for equality in education and the professions. Married women were denied many legal rights, and a woman could not act in any capacity without the consent of her husband.

Ironically, during the movement to abolish slavery in America, women were barred from many abolitionist societies. At a World Anti-slavery Convention in 1840, American women were not allowed to take part and had to sit in the balcony behind a curtain. Two women who attended the convention, Lucretia Mott and Elizabeth Cady Stanton, organized the first women's rights convention, which met in Mrs. Stanton's home in Seneca Falls, New York in July 1848. The "Declaration of Sentiments" presented at this convention was modeled after the American

Declaration of Independence. Susan B. Anthony, a dedicated and tireless promoter of the cause, joined the movement in 1851. Fredrick Douglas and Sojourner Truth, two famous black abolitionists, were also dedicated to equal rights for women.

In 1869, the Wyoming Territory was the first political body in the United States to give women the right to vote. The rest of the nation was slow to follow despite the efforts of the National American Woman Suffrage Association (NAWSA) to win the vote for women state by state. By 1912, only nine states had granted women the right to vote.

In 1912, Alice Paul and Lucy Burns returned to the United States after having been active in the British suffrage movement, which was considerably more militant than its American counterpart. Paul and Burns persuaded NAWSA to form a committee to campaign for a constitutional amendment that would grant women the right to vote.

Although President Woodrow Wilson supported suffrage privately, he would not take a public stand in favor of giving women the vote. Alice Paul's militant feminists attracted attention and growing support by picketing, through mass demonstrations, and with hunger strikes. But when NAWSA disowned the militants, they formed their own group in 1914, the Congressional Union for Women's Suffrage. In 1916, the group began to call themselves the National Women's Party.

On June 4, 1919, the 19th Amendment to the Constitution was finally passed by Congress. Carrie Chapman Catt, the president of NAWSA at the time, was an outstanding organizer. With a plan of lobbying local and state representatives and organizing women nationwide, the group helped win women the right to vote.

Warren G. Harding was the first President elected after women had the power to vote. Although he courted the women's vote during his campaign, many of them did not use their newly won power at the polls in the presidential election of 1920.

The prohibition issue had long been a controversial matter. In one Senate speech on the subject, Harding frankly admitted that he was not a "dry" (one who did not consume alcohol) and never pretended to be. "I do not approach the question from a moral viewpoint, because I am unable to see it as a great moral question." But he decided to support the 18th Amendment (which, when approved by popular vote, would make the consumption of alcohol illegal) because he thought the question should be answered "by the people who must make the ultimate decision."

CONVENTION CHAIRMAN

In 1916 Harding was asked to deliver the keynote (main) address at the Republican National Convention. He felt honored. The keynote speaker of a national political convention is looked upon by the entire country as the spokesman for his party.

The invitation to be the keynote speaker was certainly another big step forward in Harding's political career; it marked his move up to the rank of a national figure in his party. There was even some talk that perhaps Harding—with his natural talent for speaking—would be such an inspiring and commanding figure on the rostrum that "lightning would strike." The delegates would be so impressed by his speech that they would be inspired to name him the Republican presidential candidate.

But lightning did not strike Harding on the rostrum. His speech was long, lasting almost two hours. Once again, he called for party harmony and moderation. But his attempts to rouse and inspire his audience seemed to fall on deaf ears. His speech was criticized by most newspapers as being too drawn out and old-fashioned. A reporter from *The New Times* wrote, "A convention of oysters probably would compare to advantage with the animated churchyard that listened to Harding's keynote address."

Nevertheless, Harding impressed his fellow party members as a man who could be relied upon. Although his message did not set the group of delegates on fire, he was elected convention chairman. Since the Bull Moose uproar of 1912, the Progressives had lost power as a third party. Most had drifted back to join the two major parties, a majority of them aligning with the Democrats.

However, at the 1916 Republican National Convention, the Progressives were still a force to be contended with and clearly were capable of causing discord, as they had in 1912. Once again, they pushed to nominate Theodore Roosevelt. But sending a message from his home in Oyster Bay, New York, Roosevelt declined the nomination.

Two weeks after the convention, Harding made the first

gesture of conciliation with Roosevelt. In a personal, highly complimentary letter, he praised the elder statesman's sincere opposition to Wilson's re-election and his choice for party unity instead of personal interest. "I believe you will have your reward in the high opinion of your fellow countrymen," Harding wrote Roosevelt.

Like Harding, Roosevelt was never one to hold a grudge when it was politically advantageous to forgive and forget. Despite the savage attacks on Roosevelt and the Progressives that Harding had printed in the *Star,* "the great fakir" (which is what Harding called Roosevelt more than once) allowed himself to be courted and won over by the Ohio senator. Mending his fences with Roosevelt was perhaps the greatest proof of Harding's powers as a peacemaker.

In November 1916, Wilson was re-elected, defeating the Republican candidate, Charles Evan Hughes, by a very slim margin. The election was so close that it took three days to determine the winner. Nonetheless, the Democrats had come to power again, and the Republicans felt it was time to rally and regroup. Following Wilson's re-election, Teddy Roosevelt (who was now the obvious Republican leader and presidential candidate for 1920) invited Harding to a conference where top party members would meet to discuss how to rebuild the Republican Party.

Despite his success at reconciliation with Roosevelt, the poor response to his keynote address was a great disappointment to Harding. Ever since his school days, Harding had always been proud of his talent for public speaking. Yet, when all eyes were upon him for what was perhaps his most important opportunity to prove himself, he floundered. The big city newspapers all over the country had given his performance poor reviews. It all seemed a bad omen for whatever hopes he now had of eventually capturing the presidential nomination himself someday.

Chapter 5

"The Day Has Come"

When Warren Harding arrived in Washington in 1915, the country was alert to the threat of war. The war in Europe between the Central Powers (Germany, Austria-Hungary, Bulgaria, and Turkey) and the Allied Powers (mainly France and England) had begun in August 1914. President Wilson stood firm in his belief that the United States should remain neutral, and the majority of the country seemed to agree with him. However, for a long time America had enjoyed good relationships with the democratic governments of England and France. U.S. ties to the more militaristic and undemocratic Central Powers were considerably weaker.

As the war continued, Americans began to believe that the country had an obligation to help the Allies. Although the United States had not yet sent soldiers to fight on European soil, its financial investment in the war was growing. By 1917 American banks had lent the Allies $1.5 billion. While Germany was blockaded by the British fleet and restricted from trading with the United States, this money was used by the Allies to buy American goods.

THE *LUSITANIA* INCIDENT

In May 1915, the *Lusitania,* a British ship carrying a number of American civilians, was attacked and sunk by a German submarine off the coast of Ireland. Many thought for sure that this loss of American lives would be the final rallying cry for a declaration of war against Germany. It seemed inevitable that the United States would now enter the European conflict, but President Wilson still hung back.

After the *Lusitania* incident, Theodore Roosevelt and others who had long thought that the United States should enter the war were even more critical of Wilson's reluctance to send troops to help the Allies. Roosevelt and others urged the government to prepare America to fight. In October 1915, Harding had occasion to express his views in the Senate on the matter. He spoke in favor of American preparedness, saying he thought the country should double the size of the Army. However, doing his best not to antagonize those who supported Wilson, Harding took a much more moderate tone than Roosevelt about entering the war, saying it was unwise to "rush to militarism."

Maintaining Neutrality

Yet, America still held to a policy of neutrality. In 1916 Wilson was re-elected President on a stance of noninvolvement and the campaign slogan, " He Kept Us Out of War." However, his popularity was declining and he barely defeated Charles Evans Hughes to win a second term in the White House. Soon after Wilson's re-election, it looked as if the German Kaiser might be willing to negotiate peace with the Allies. But the Allies were unwilling to negotiate with Germany.

As Wilson tried to orchestrate the proper diplomatic forum for peace talks, Germany once more took an antagonistic position and stepped up its warfare. The Imperial German government declared that, as of February 1, 1917, the German Navy would blockade all access to the Mediterranean, the French coast, and the British Isles and resume unrestricted submarine warfare.

WILSON'S WAR RESOLUTION

Shocked and disappointed by this new turn of events, Wilson appeared before Congress two days later to announce a break in all diplomatic relations with Germany. A group of congressmen opposed to America's involvement in the war blocked a resolution that would arm American merchant ships. They managed to keep the question from coming to a vote by a filibuster (prolonged speeches purposefully obstructing the vote on a resolution). But when the session ended on March 3, Wilson used his authority as President to arm the nation's merchant ships.

German submarines continued to attack neutral vessels, sinking 750,000 tons of shipping a month. Wilson was finally pushed to enter the war when three American merchant ships— the *City of Memphis,* the *Illinois* and the *Vigilancia*— were torpedoed on March 18. On April 2, Wilson called a special session of Congress and requested a declaration of war against Germany.

Four days later, Wilson's war resolution was passed by both the Senate and the House of Representatives. Although Harding had wavered earlier, he now supported the war resolution, debating in its favor on the Senate floor. Only five senators voted against the resolution.

The Roosevelt Amendment

Theodore Roosevelt was eager to lead a division of American volunteers to Europe immediately. When a draft bill was being drawn up in the Senate that would require all men between the ages of 21 and 30 to serve in the armed forces, Harding tried his best to help his party leader by adding an amendment to the bill. The amendment would allow Roosevelt to raise his volunteer units. When the draft bill was passed by both Houses, it included Harding's "Roosevelt" amendment.

However, when Wilson signed the bill, he made it clear that he would not approve the formation of any volunteer divisions. He did so despite the fact that Roosevelt had already opened a recruiting center in New York City and 200,000 applicants had volunteered to serve with him. Wilson tried to refuse Roosevelt's wishes gracefully, saying that sending the former President's group to Europe would be a compliment to the Allies and a "poetic" gesture. But truthfully, Wilson believed that Roosevelt — like most Americans — was working from a knowledge of warfare that was dangerously outdated.

THE WAR EFFORT

The war effort began on a large scale, with the government taking control of many aspects of the economy. Both the public and private industry had to follow government directives as never before in the country's history. The money needed to fight the war was raised with heavy taxes and through the sale of war bonds called Liberty Loans. A fighting force was drafted, ships were built to combat German submarines, and the government took control of the railroads away from private owners.

Food and fuel were rationed under the direction of Herbert Hoover, who would later become the 31st President of the United States. Hoover's efforts were so successful that "Hooverizing" came to mean economizing. In the meantime, the War Industries Board put the country's factories to work producing the goods needed to equip the armed forces.

About a year and a half after the draft bill was approved, an army of four million men had been trained and equipped.

The American Navy had also been built up to an impressive fighting force. By the fall of 1918, about two million Americans had joined the Allies on the battlefields of Europe.

Helpful Hardings

During this time, Harding was assigned to the Naval Affairs Committee, the Committee on the Philippines, and the Committee on Standards, Weights and Measures. He also offered to help Hoover in any way he could. He voted for food and fuel control, believing that, in the country's crisis, Wilson should be given full power as President to do as he saw fit.

Florence Harding also did her patriotic duty by participating with other senators' wives in a sewing circle that met in the Senate office building. The sewing circle kept Florence quite busy. Her health had improved considerably since the Hardings had first moved to Washington, and with all the old energy of her days in the *Star* offices, she kept very active. When the war started, Flossie did not even know how to work a sewing machine. But she now spent six to seven hours a day, several days a week, sewing clothes for war orphans.

The President's Daughter

At about this time, Harding became romantically involved with Nan Britton, a young woman who was 22 years his junior. Nan had grown up in Marion, where Harding had been friends with her father, Dr. Samuel Britton. When she was a teenager, Nan's schoolgirl crush on Marion's leading citizen was no secret to her girlfriends and neighbors.

Their relationship began in the summer of 1917, when Nan was about 20 and living in New York. She wrote to Harding in Washington, asking if he remembered her from Marion and also wondering if the senator could help her find better employment. Despite his subsequent involvement with Nan, Harding still continued a strained relationship and correspondence with Carrie Phillips, up until the time of his presidential campaign in 1920.

In October 1919, Nan Britton gave birth to Harding's only child, which she named Elizabeth Ann. The baby was born in Asbury Park, New Jersey. Nan and the child soon moved to Chicago, where Nan's sister lived.

At Harding's suggestion, Elizabeth Ann was adopted by Nan's sister and brother-in-law, Elizabeth and Scott Willits. Harding partially supported Nan and gave the Willits $500 a month for the child's needs. However, he took no further interest in his daughter and never saw more than a photograph of her.

Harding's relationship with Nan Britton continued during his presidency. After his death, she wrote a book about their relationship. Entitled *The President's Daughter,* the manuscript was rejected by a number of publishers. But Nan finally managed to have it published privately in 1927, and it soon became a best-seller. Nan donated the book's profits to the Elizabeth Ann League, a charity organization she founded for unwed mothers and their children.

ALLIED VICTORY

The war ended on November 11, 1918. As American troops returned from Europe, they were welcomed home with parades up Fifth Avenue in New York City. Now that the United States had "made the world safe for democracy," Wilson hoped to negotiate terms for a peace that would protect all nations against future wars.

In January of 1918, Wilson outlined for Congress 14 measures he hoped would ensure world peace. He also wanted to establish a "general association of nations" that would be dedicated to keeping that peace and protecting "political independence and territorial integrity." This association was to be known as the League of Nations, a forerunner of the existing United Nations.

At Versailles, a town in France not far from Paris, the Allies — the United States, France, and Great Britain — met with German representatives to draft a peace treaty. The Treaty of Versailles included Wilson's 14 measures for ensuring world peace, admission of German war guilt, and promises by Germany to pay an unspecified amount of money to the Allies to aid in rebuilding the war-ravaged nations. The treaty also included a clause for founding the League of Nations.

THE LEAGUE OF NATIONS BATTLE

President Wilson was very dedicated to establishing the League of Nations. But when he brought the signed peace treaty home to be ratified (approved) by the Senate, senators were divided over the question of establishing the League. It was in this battle between Wilson and the Senate over the League of Nations that Warren Harding first truly made a name for himself.

The Senate was split into four camps over the League of Nations issue. One group consisted of Wilson's staunch supporters, who urged that the treaty be ratified without any changes or compromises. Another group consisted of isolationists, who still believed — despite the war that had just been fought and won — that the United States should remain aloof from world politics. They wanted the League clause completely removed from the treaty. A third group would accept the League with some minor compromises, and a fourth would accept the League with stricter compromises.

Massachusetts Senator Henry Cabot Lodge, the chairman of the Senate's powerful Foreign Relations Committee, was a vocal and bitter opponent of Wilson on this issue. Lodge claimed to be in the group that would accept the treaty with some strict limitations. He rallied others, Harding among them, to fight what many considered to be Wilson's arrogance, high-handedness, and his attempt to abuse presidential power.

An Unwise Move

Wilson's relationship with the Senate — even his supporters — had grown strained when he had chosen not to take any senators — either Democratic or Republican, to travel with him as advisors to the peace negotiations in Versailles. This had been unwise of Wilson, because he knew that a treaty negotiated by the executive branch had to be ratified by the Senate. Choosing some senators from both parties to aid in the negotiations would have given Wilson congressional allies at this critical time.

Now, Wilson was insisting publicly that the treaty be ratified by the Senate without any changes. His supporters begged him to compromise, but he would not. His stubborn position infuriated such opponents as Henry Cabot Lodge even further.

Harding's Objections

Lodge was trying to enlist all Republican senators to take a stand against Wilson, and Harding aligned himself with the anti-League group. But Harding had his own thoughts about the issue. He wrote to a friend at this time, "My own judgement is that in the long run this country will be very hostile to this venture into the unknown."

Another reason why Harding took a strong stand against the League was because he belived that his constituents, the Ohio citizens he represented, were against it. Also, by the time the issue came to a final vote in the Senate, he believed the popular opinion of the whole country had turned against the League plan that Wilson insisted should remain unchanged.

In mid-August, Harding and a group of other senators called on Wilson at the White House to discuss their differences over the League. Harding confronted Wilson with a question about an article in the plan, which stated that the commitment of nations who joined the League would be only a moral and not a legal one. Harding asked Wilson how world peace would be maintained if the binding obligation were only moral and not legal. Wilson sidestepped the question twice, but Harding did not forget the point. In a major speech before the Senate on September 11, 1919, Harding voiced his doubts about Wilson's plan and again pointed out his objections to the commitment article, which he saw as a major flaw.

Harding's question about the League (a legal versus moral commitment) and its potential to be an effective governing body that would maintain world peace was a valid one. Years later, just before his death, Harding would return to this question when he proposed that the United States should join the World Court.

Defeat of the League

Despite what his opponents in the Senate said, Wilson still believed that most Americans wanted the United States to join the League of Nations. He decided to go on a speaking tour in the late summer of 1919 to bring his message to the people. Traveling by train nearly 10,000 miles through the Middle and Far West, his schedule was exhausting. His health was already poor from the strain of his role as Commander-in-Chief during the war. The many months he had spent in Europe working on the peace treaty and fighting the Senate had also taken their toll.

As Wilson traveled from town to town, his Republican opponents sent out groups to heckle and badger him during his speeches. Although Harding was opposed to the League, he admired Wilson's courage and persistence and did not approve of the harassment.

In Pueblo, Colorado, towards the end of September, President Wilson collapsed from exhaustion. Back in Washington a few days later, he had a serious stroke that kept him bedridden and unable to work for months. He was never again physically capable to meet the demands of his office. His long battle with the Senate was over.

In November the Senate put the treaty to a vote. One group defeated it without reservations, and another with reservations, which meant the Senate might approve it if certain changes were made. In March 1920, the treaty was put to vote again, and again it was defeated. Nevertheless, the issue remained alive and was given more attention during the presidential campaign in 1920, but by that time most Americans were no longer interested in the question. They wanted to put the war behind them and get on with their lives.

Chapter 6

From the Front Porch to the White House

When Theodore Roosevelt died in January 1919, America mourned the passing of one of the greatest statesmen of the century. In the Republican Party, the aging Rough Rider had still been a powerful, central force, His absence left a great gap in party leadership.

It was well known that Roosevelt wanted to run again in the upcoming presidential election. As the acknowledged leader of his party, the former President had been working since 1916 to repair the split caused by the Progressives in 1912. The reunited Republican Party was perhaps finally ready to stand behind Roosevelt as a presidential candidate in 1920. Most believed that he would have no real competition for the nomination within the party.

AN OPEN FIELD

However, with Roosevelt gone, the field was now wide open. Many Republicans who had not seriously considered putting their name up against Roosevelt now thought they might have a chance to win the nomination. Harding was just such a presidential hopeful. He wrote to an old friend at home, "The death of Col. Roosevelt will somewhat change the plans of some Republicans in Ohio." He hoped that Roosevelt's supporters in Ohio would now stand behind him as the Republican presidential candidate.

Harding came to the Republican National Convention in Chicago with only a few delegates pledged to vote for him. But many more had agreed that if there was a deadlock, he would be their second choice. As the nominating process dragged on, a stalemate developed between the two front runners, General Leonard Wood and Frank O. Lowden. It was at this time that Harding won the exciting nomination on the tenth ballot in an unexpected swell of delegate support.

The Logical Choice

Harding was humble and grateful as he accepted the great honor his party had bestowed upon him. Only a few months before, he had been considered by many to be an impossible candidate, but somehow he had emerged as the logical choice.

In the days following the convention, Harding did strike most everyone as a good choice for the Republican nomination. People would say he even looked, acted, and talked like a President. The Republican newspapers quickly endorsed his candidacy. *The Atlanta* (Georgia) *Constitution* wrote, "As for Senator Harding, he will unquestionably make a strong candidate. . . . The Republicans might have gone further and done much worse."

Years later, when scandals and corruption were uncovered in Harding's administration, many would forget how well his candidacy had been received. Some would assert that the night before the nomination, Harding and his campaign manager, Harry Daugherty, made certain deals with political bosses and business leaders in order to "buy" the delegate votes. However, most accounts of the day report that the un-expected shift of delegates to Harding was a result of the Wood-Lowden stalemate and the spontaneous choice of the delegates themselves.

THE FRONT PORCH CAMPAIGN

Returning to Marion, Ohio, in late June, Harding received a hero's welcome. The Civic Association had renamed the street from Union Depot to the Harding home as "Victory Way" and decorated it with white columns and gold eagles for over a mile. The windows in nearly every storefront in town displayed giant posters of Harding draped with red, white, and blue bunting.

The afternoon the Hardings returned to Marion from Washington, they found several hundred of their neighbors, friends, and admirers waiting in front of their house on Mount Vernon Avenue. It was not long before news of their return had spread and the crowd swelled to 3,000. Harding greeted the people and read a speech. Then he presented his wife, "the Duchess," whom he called "a good scout who knows all my faults and yet has stuck to me all the way."

And so began Harding's presidential campaign, most of it conducted from the front porch of his home. At the Demo-cratic National Convention in San Francisco, Ohio's Gover-nor James Cox was nominated to run against him. Cox hit the campaign trail and "stumped" around the country to speak to voters. Harding, on the other hand, chose to spend most of the campaign months at home in Marion.

The friendly house, built when the Hardings were first married, was painted green with white trim. The porch had been rebuilt and widened in 1899, when it collapsed under the weight of well-wishers who greeted Harding after he was elected to the Ohio Senate. It was the perfect place from which to run a presidential campaign; it now ran the entire length of the house, extending out in a large round deck, something like a bandstand.

Campaign Strategy

Harding's campaign strategy followed in the tradition of one of his personal heroes, Ohio-born President William McKinley, who had also run a successful presidential campaign from his home in 1896. For good luck, the Hardings had the flagpole from McKinley's home in Canton, Ohio, moved to their own front yard. The flag was raised each morning at seven o'clock, sometimes by Harding himself. The yard was now covered with gravel so that the visiting crowds and marching bands would not trample the ground to mud.

Speaking from his own front porch in his own hometown, Harding was the very picture of dignity, sincerity, and respectability. In comparison to Cox, whom one observer noted was "campaigning all over the lot, in a sweat," Harding's image was that of "a quiet gentleman." In the eye of the American voter, he seemed to represent essential American values like neighborliness, cooperation, and hard work.

In comparison to the scholarly Wilson, the public identified with Harding's image as an "average man." He was a self-made person from a small town who was not visionary, but practical. Moreover, he was a man who could supply some common sense cures to heal postwar wounds.

Harding began the campaign officially on a Saturday afternoon in late July, addressing about 2,000 factory workers, businessmen, and farmers who had come to hear him from

Presidential candidate Warren Harding (center) with Republican Party leader Will Hays (left) and vice-presidential candidate Calvin Coolidge (right) in October 1920. Harding's campaign strategy struck the right note with American voters. (Library of Congress.)

Ohio's Richland County. By the end of September, over 600,000 people had come to Marion to listen and even to speak to Harding personally.

Flossie's Support

Flossie Harding was also a great help to her husband during the campaign even though she had once opposed his wish to run for President. But right before the convention in Chicago, when his campaign seemed lost and he was ready to give up, she had urged him to fight until the bitter end.

Campaigning in Marion, Flossie seemed to thrive on the excitement, the speeches, and the parades. She did not appear to mind the crowds that filled her house and front yard to overflowing. Groups that came to Mount Vernon Avenue— the Elks, the Moose, the Ohio State Dental Association— always greeted her name with applause. The press liked her and the women voters—now an important group—approved of her as well. Throughout the summer, she kept in touch with her friends in Washington, particularly Evalyn MacLean, to whom she wrote, "No matter what comes into my life I shall always regard this summer as one of the greatest epochs."

At the end of September, Harding and his campaign advisors decided it was time for him to leave his front porch and hit the campaign trail. Traveling by train, he spoke in Maryland, West Virginia, and Kentucky. Then in October, he toured the Midwest, including Iowa, Missouri, and Oklahoma. He also made a one-day trip to Buffalo and Syracuse in upstate New York.

CAMPAIGN ISSUES

When Harding went out to meet American voters in the fall of 1920, the nation's mood was uneasy and deflated. The war was over, although not "technically" resolved in regard to the treaties still to be ratified and the League of Nations issue. But where was the country headed? President Wilson was seriously ill and the White House was silent. There were even rumors that Wilson was deranged or in a coma, and that his wife and a few advisors were really running the country.

The end of the war had caused shifts in the economy. When soldiers returned home, they found a housing shortage, because the war effort had temporarily halted most building construction. It was also hard for veterans to find jobs. There were business failures, and umemployment rose to over four million. Industries reduced hours and wages.

On Wall Street, trading on the New York Stock Exchange was brisk, even busier than before the war. Stocks were on the rise, but many felt the trend would not last, and business would soon be facing a postwar depression. They were right;

in June 1920 the market went flat. In the Midwest, farmers were suffering from a severe drop in the price of wheat. In 1919, wheat had sold for $2.15 a bushel, but now the price had dropped to 88 cents.

There was also discord between business and labor, resulting in major strikes. In January 1919, union leaders in Seattle, Washington, called a general strike to support ship-yard workers. A few months later, the Boston police went on strike. Many citizens, however, were not sympathetic to the grievances of the unions. They considered the strikes anti-American and led by "radical" agitators.

The Red Scare

Suspicion of labor activists was part of the great social un-rest in the years following World War I. Along with the patri-otic fervor of wartime had come a suspicion of anyone who spoke out against government policies. Foreign-born Ameri-cans were now particularly suspect. Even though the United States was essentially a nation of immigrants, some families could trace their ancestors back several generations to early Anglo-Saxon arrivals. They considered themselves "native" Americans.

But many families had come to the United States more recently from such European countries as Poland, Germany, and Italy. There was strong popular feeling in the country that immigration should be restricted. Americans no longer welcomed the "huddled masses yearning to breathe free" (as inscribed on the Statue of Liberty) with open arms, as had been the policy in the early part of the century.

The Russian Revolution in the fall of 1918 also contrib-uted to America's unrest. In a violent upheaval, the Commu-nists took control of the Russian government. Founded on the political philosophy of Karl Marx, the Communist Party was dedicated to establishing a society in which, unlike capitalism, there is no private ownership of property, and the government controls the production and distribution of all goods.

Americans wondered: If it could happen in Russia, could it not happen here? The unstable economy and lack of strong leadership in the White House seemed to make some people feel as if the country was ripe for revolution. A small Communist Party had already been organized in the United States. Many people were unjustly suspected of being "Red," "radical," or part of a conspiracy to undermine the United States government. Their homes were raided and their civil rights were denied. No plot to overthrow the government was ever uncovered, and these years were later referred to as the "Red Scare."

The American public was ready for a change from Democratic leadership. Whether it was fair or not, most voters blamed Wilson and the Democratic party for the nation's present troubles. Harding's calm, hopeful message was just what they wanted to hear.

A Desire for Normalcy

Harding's message to the voters was clear. He understood their postwar problems and anxieties. He seemed to be a calm, reliable statesman who could lead the country back to normalcy. In a speech in Boston before he won the nomination in Chicago, Harding said, "America's present need is not heroics but healing; not nostrums [questionable remedies] but normalcy; not revolution but restoration; not surgery but serenity."

Throughout his campaign, Harding would repeat this message of healing and promote the return to a peaceful, more prosperous era. Wilson was associated with a spirit of internationalism and idealism. Under his leadership, Americans had fought and died to defend the freedom of other nations. Now that the war was over, many thought the entire effort had been senseless. Recuperating from the war, Americans felt more nationalistic, more concerned with the problems within the United States than those in foreign lands.

Harding's call to put "America First" struck just the right note with the voters. Speaking in New York in January 1920, he first touched upon the slogan that would be repeated throughout his campaign and carried into his administration. "Let the internationalist dream and the Bolshevist [Russian Communist] destroy," he said. (The "internationalist dream" was a reference to Wilson and his admirable but impractical "dream" of a League of Nations.)

Harding then went on to outline his own program for the country, saying it was time:

> To safeguard America first;
> To stabilize America first;
> To prosper America first;
> To think of America first;
> To exalt America first;
> To live for and revere America first.

Critics were quick to point out that Harding's patriotic "laundry list" lacked specific suggestions as to how he would make the country more stable and prosperous. But what his campaign rhetoric lacked in details he more than made up for with comforting, positive-sounding, patriotic phrases that appealed to the average citizen. To many, "America First" sounded like the exact opposite of Wilson's policies. It was time for America to put its own house in order and return to a policy of political (though not necessarily economic) isolation.

Promises and Programs

While campaigning, Harding did speak about some specific ways in which he would solve the country's problems. If elected President, he promised to establish a temporary emergency tariff that would give farmers some immediate relief until a permanent high tariff could be established. At this time, he also spoke in favor of increased credit for farmers. However, once he took office, his administration did not adopt a policy of encouraging banks to help farmers.

In regard to labor, Harding took the middle ground. He seemed to support unionism and collective bargaining (negotiations between unions and employers to settle issues) but opposed the idea of labor having more say in the running of business or government. Although Harding did not take a hardline, antilabor stand, he was not in favor of legislation or policies that would give unions real power.

As a help to business and workers, Harding proposed restructuring the tax system and lowering taxes on private incomes. Lower taxes was certainly good news for the voters. Although Harding did follow through on this proposal after he was elected President, the new tax system that resulted was not quite what most voters had hoped for.

All over the country, people were economizing. Harding saw the need for government to tighten its belt, too, and cut back on spending. During his campaign, he promised that he would initiate a budget system for controlling federal spending. He was the first President to propose such a program and then follow through on it with considerable success.

In keeping with popular sentiment, Harding also favored tighter immigration laws that would limit the number of immigrants permitted to enter the United States annually. He courted the black vote and spoke in favor of antilynching laws, the protection of constitutional rights for blacks, and the appointment of more blacks to government at federal and local levels.

The "League" Question: A Big Campaign Issue

The League of Nations question was a sore point for Harding during his campaign. From his sickbed, President Wilson still tried to push the issue. The Democratic candidate, James Cox, also spoke in favor of America joining the League. When Harding spoke about his position on foreign relations and the League question during the campaign, he seemed to contradict his earlier position. This wavering made him an easy target for both Cox and the press.

Earlier that year in the Senate, Harding had clearly sided with the anti-League group, headed by Henry Cabot Lodge. But during his campaign, he shocked and angered these fellow Republicans and also caused a stir in the press when he appeared to reverse his anti-League position.

In Favor of a World Court

Speaking from his front porch in Marion on August 28, Harding said that he did not favor America joining the League as outlined by Wilson at Versailles. But he did believe that the United States could help maintain world peace by taking part in some international organization—no matter what it was called: "I believe humanity would welcome the creation of an international association for conference and a world court whose verdicts upon justiciable questions [those capable of being decided by a court of justice], this country in common with all nations would be both willing and able to uphold."

In October, Harding again clarified his position for the press on the League of Nations issue. At that time he said that he was opposed to the League as defined in Paris, and he was definitely in favor of a "world association — call it what you will . . . that will discourage or tend to prevent war." The notion of some international peacekeeping association was not just empty campaign rhetoric, but stayed with Harding after his election. A desire for America to join a world court was the focus of his last cross-country speaking tour.

At the time, many thought Harding's views would hurt him with the voters. Popular sentiment was largely against the League and America playing a role of any kind in international politics. Republican leaders advised him to take a clear anti-League stand and avoid saying anything more about the issue of international associations.

Cox thought he could discredit Harding and make him look foolish to the voters by drawing attention to Harding's contradictions. However, Harding's overall appeal to the voters was much stronger than Cox — or even his fellow Republicans — realized. By focusing on the League of Nations issue during the campaign, Cox actually soured his own image with voters, for they began to identify him with Wilson, about whom they had very negative feelings at this time.

HAPPY BIRTHDAY, W.G.

Harding's popularity grew stronger every day during his campaign. In July his odds at winning the election were figured to be only two to one. But by November, it looked like he had a ten-to-one chance of winning, the highest for any presidential election up to that time.

On election day, November 2, 1920, the Hardings voted in the morning and then the candidate went to play golf in Columbus with his campaign manager, Harry Daugherty. When Harding returned home that evening, he found a sur-

Florence and Warren Harding spent election day, November 6, 1920, at home in Marion, Ohio. They read returns and celebrated Harding's 55th birthday. That night, the entire town surrounded their house to celebrate Harding's landslide victory. (Library of Congress.)

prise birthday party waiting for him. With close friends, family, and his wife cheering him on, he blew out the 55 pink candles on his birthday cake. Everybody knew what he wished for.

Along with the many well-wishers, a group of employees from the *Star* came by to deliver a special birthday gift to their publisher, whom they fondly called "W.G." Harding met them himself on the porch and opened his present. It was another make-up rule, exactly like the one he had received from Will Warner and still carried in his pocket for good luck. This one was cast in solid gold and engraved with the date of the election on one side and an optimistic blank spot for the date of his possible re-election in 1924 as well.

Harding was very moved and had tears in his eyes as he expressed his gratitude. He told the group, "I am coming into a position of great responsibility, if the present returns are interpreted correctly. I have been on the square with you, and I want to be on the square with all the world."

A LANDSLIDE VICTORY

Harding's secretary, George Christian, lived next door. Telephone and telegraph equipment had been set up in the Christian kitchen to receive the election results. Before midnight, it was clear that Harding's birthday wish had come true. He had won the election by a landslide. Crowds flocked to the Hardings' front porch and filled Mount Vernon Avenue. The town celebrated the victory of their leading citizen all night long, as if it were New Year's Eve. Flossie and Warren Harding did not go to bed themselves until five in the morning.

Harding won the election with 60.2 percent of the popular vote, the largest popular majority for a President that had so far been recorded in the country's history. In every section of the country except the South, Harding's popular vote exceeded 60 percent and went as high as 65 percent in the Midwest and New England. The final tally was 16,181,289 votes for Harding, 9,141,750 for Cox, and 941,827 for Eugene V. Debs, a labor leader and Socialist candidate who was currently serving a prison term for antiwar activities. Harding received 404 electoral votes to Cox's 127, winning 37 of the 48 states. He also had the distinction of being the first man to be elevated from the U.S. Senate directly into the White House.

Hit by an Earthquake

Harding had been expected to win big, but the actual margin of his victory surpassed even the wildest dreams of Republicans and the darkest nightmares of Democrats. One Republican called it "the most joyous thing that ever happened," while on the Democratic side, it was said, "It wasn't a landslide, it was an earthquake." Franklin Delano Roosevelt, who had been Cox's running mate and who would later become President himself, said to one of his associates, "Thank God we are both comparatively youthful."

Some historians have stated that Harding's tremendous victory was not the expression of the voter's love for him, but the voter's dislike for Wilson. World War I had marked a new era in the nation's history. A vote for Harding and the Republican ticket was an expression of America's desire to clean house in Washington, D.C., and bring in new men for the new era.

Chapter 7

The Gates Swing Open

In his inauguration address on March 4, 1921, Harding told his fellow Americans, "Our supreme task is the resumption of our onward, normal way. Reconstruction, readjustment, restoration — all these must follow."

In his first address to the country as President, Harding repeated his campaign themes of a "return to normalcy" and "America first." He also spoke about the nation's most urgent postwar problems, particularly economic recovery. Two remedies he planned to enact were reducing high taxes that prevailed during the war and controlling government spending.

Harding warned Americans that there would be difficult times ahead, that wage reductions would come before "a rigid and yet sane economy" could be achieved. But in his typically optimistic and confident style, he added that the outlook was more than hopeful, and that an eventual upswing in the natural cycle of business was inevitable. He also struck a distinctly probusiness note when he said he spoke for "the omission of unnecessary interference of government with business" and "for an end of government's experiment in business."

On Inauguration Day March 4, 1921, the ailing, outgoing President Woodrow Wilson (left) rode with Harding (second from the left) in an open carriage. Two members of Congress rode up front. (Library of Congress.)

A CLEAR MESSAGE

Harding's inaugural address was generally well received by the press and public. *The New York Times* observed that the speech confirmed the popular impression of the new President—that he was a man who did not pretend to possess "uncommon wisdom" but "whose intentions are of the best, who is sincerely anxious to make his Presidency useful and safe, rather than brilliant." This last comparison was perhaps a reference to Wilson, who did aspire to leave a mark of brilliance in the world's history books with his League of Nations plan.

For the average American, Harding's inaugural speech

once again struck the right note. His style of speaking was much more flowery and wordy than Wilson's crisp sentences. In fact, a writer once compared Harding's speaking style to "a string of wet sponges." But the new President's practical solutions, backed by his steady optimism, was a clear message that everyone could understand. One woman in the crowd was heard to say afterward, "We have had Wilson eight years, and I have not understood him. I understand Harding already."

Meeting with the Senate

Immediately after being sworn in as President, Harding walked over to the Senate chamber to personally present the names of the men he had chosen for his Cabinet. Although once a tradition, it was now unusual for the President to meet with the Senate on the day of his inauguration. Harding was the first President to do so since Thomas Jefferson.

The senators greeted their former colleague with a round of applause. They most likely had the impression that they would not be at odds with this new President—one of their own—as they had been with Wilson.

Each President comes into office with some idea of how he will interpret that office and his powers as chief executive under the Constitution. It was the general consensus that Harding would not try to dominate the Senate and would assume only as much power as the legislative branch of government and constitutional limits would allow. Some wrongly assumed Harding would willingly be controlled by the Senate.

As might have been predicted, Harding's message to his former colleagues was a wish for a future cooperative relationship. But he made it clear on that day that he did not plan to give up his rights as President to the Senate. He did not believe that the legislative branch of government should try to challenge or trespass on the executive branch. As he had once said, "Our [the Senate's] highest duty is the preservation of the constituted powers of each [the executive and legislative branches of the government], and the promotion of the spirit of cooperation so essential to our common welfare."

The Senate was required to approve the President's Cabinet members, a procedure that often involved weeks of debate and investigation into each proposed Cabinet member's background and qualifications. Harding's Cabinet choices were greeted with applause by the Senate and quickly approved.

A BREATH OF FRESH AIR

When Warren G. Harding entered the White House, his wish was not to go down in history as a great President. He hoped instead to be remembered as America's "best-loved" President. From the moment he set foot in Washington as the President-elect, the mood in the nation's capital seemed lightened and more optimistic.

Ever since Wilson had delivered his war message, the iron gates to the White House had been locked, barred, and watched over by an armed guard. During his presidency, the White House had always been remote from the public and characterized by an atmosphere of icy decorum. After he became ill, the building was virtually deserted, the hush and stillness of the sickroom permeating throughout. Although Wilson was a strong leader and admired as a scholar, a visionary, and an intellectual, he had always held himself at a distance from the American public.

Harding, however, quickly sought to surround himself with the people who had voted for him. If he is not recalled as the President people loved most, he was certainly one who most-loved people. Almost as if he were still trying to win votes, he carried the tone of his front porch campaign into the capital.

Off to a Positive Start

As soon as Harding returned to the White House from his inauguration, he ordered the iron gates thrown open. Later that day, when the open gates had attracted a group of curious citizens, Florence Harding found the servants closing the curtains in the White House East Room. She insisted that the curtains remain open. "Let 'em look if they want to," she said. "It's their White House."

Harding insisted on keeping the inauguration ceremonies simple because of the widespread economic depression and his pledge to reduce federal spending. "I believe most heartily in a practical keeping of the faith from the very beginning," he said. There was a small parade, but no publicly sponsored ball. Evalyn and Ned MacLean, the Hardings' close friends, hosted a private party for select members of the new administration and foreign officials at their Washington estate. The press and public approved of this restraint and felt the new President was getting off to a positive start.

But even with the gates on the White House open wide and the curtains drawn back, the Hardings were not merely content to have Americans look in from the outside. The day after the inauguration, the lower floors and the grounds of the White House were open to visitors for the first time in many years.

Florence Harding set about brightening up the presidential mansion's rather drab atmosphere. There were changes made in the decor, both inside and out. The Hardings had always liked to entertain their friends, and continued to do so in their new home on Pennsylvania Avenue. Flossie added more colorful interior decorations and flowers in almost every room. Gardeners set to work planting thousands of bulbs on the White House lawns, and birdhouses were tacked up in the trees. Mrs. Harding hosted three garden parties for war veterans that summer and revived the tradition of White House teas. Once again, there was an "Easter Egg Roll" for children on the south grounds and Marine Band concerts on the lawn.

A People-Loving President

Harding would come out of his office each day between 12:30 and lunch to meet and chat with visitors. These sessions usually lasted about 15 minutes, sometimes longer. Sometimes as many as 2,000 people would be there, hoping to shake hands with their friendly new President.

Teachers and school children, club and lodge members, tourists, foreigners, religious groups, baseball and football teams, movie stars—Harding was happy to meet them all. The First Lady would join him from time to time, or he would bring along his dog, Laddie Boy, a friendly Airedale terrier.

Despite the objections of his personal secretary, George Christian, Harding insisted that meeting with White House visitors was a worthwhile part of his day. "I love to meet people," Harding insisted. "It is the most pleasant thing I do; it is really the only fun I have."

Relations with the Press

If meeting visitors was the favorite part of Harding's day, meeting with reporters had to be a close second. Shortly after Harding took office, it was clear that he would have one of the best relationships with the press of any President in history.

Once again, Harding was the complete opposite of Wilson in the way he treated newspaper reporters. Wilson had disliked regular White House news conferences. When he did meet with reporters, it was with a carefully prepared statement and rarely on a free, give-and-take basis.

Harding, on the other hand, felt a strong kinship with newsmen, having been one himself. And having owned a newspaper, he also understood the power of the press to help or hinder his presidency. He understood their work and did not treat them with distrust or antagonism. He did not speak to reporters in the high-handed manner that some Presidents assumed, nor did he ignore them. He knew many newsmen by their first name and often referred to the press corps that covered the White House as "our newspaper family."

At his very first news conference, President Harding welcomed reporters to the White House, meeting them personally at the door and shaking each one's hand. Then, leaning back on a desktop amid the group, he spoke to them casually without waiting for questions. In his press conferences he was very open and honest about problems he faced as the President, and did not try to hide his flaws and limitations. He was also very open, though not indiscreet, about what went on behind the scenes in his administration. The press had perhaps never before been privy to such a revealing look at the presidency.

Personal Amusements

Once in the White House, the private life of a President and his family is closely watched by the public. Many of Harding's personal tastes and habits were criticized after his death and after the scandals in his administration became public. Also criticized later and greatly exaggerated were the amount of time Harding spent "relaxing" and the influence of his companions. But while he was in the White House, not many considered his enjoyment of golf and card playing objectionable or found that Harding spent any more time in these personal pursuits than did other Presidents.

Harding played golf about twice a week. His time on the golf course was less, in fact, than Wilson spent golfing weekly before his stroke. Although Harding loved golf with a passion, he was not very good at it. Nevertheless, he played competitively and liked to bet. The press frequently photographed him on the course, often with his dog, Laddie Boy, whom he had trained to retrieve his practice balls.

Harding also liked to play poker. As a senator, he had played almost every Saturday night. After becoming President, he would invite both friends and members of the government to a card game in his study about twice a week. The games would start after dinner and break up about midnight. Florence Harding and Evalyn MacLean were also usually present, although Mrs. Harding did not play cards herself.

After the administration fell into disgrace, it was said that Harding's "poker Cabinet" was really running the government, or that secret plans were made during these games to rob the taxpayers blind. Doubtlessly, some official business was discussed at these gatherings. But Harding enjoyed these hours as a break from the pressures of his office, not as special advisory sessions. He was not the first or the last President to play cards in the White House. The card games were more an indication of Harding's interests rather than an unofficial Cabinet that was running the country.

Breaking the Law

The Volstead Act, which Harding had voted for in the Senate, made the sale and consumption of liquor illegal as of January 1, 1920. It was known, however, that Harding served liquor in the private rooms of the White House and drank himself, although liquor was not served at public gatherings in the social rooms on the first floor.

Many Americans were not in favor of prohibition and did not observe the law. Harding himself drank moderately and believed that what he did in his own private quarters was his own business. However, even as President, he was breaking the law. Even if his office gave him "unofficial" protection from law enforcement, it did not protect him from gossip and criticism.

Later in his administration, in 1922, Harding made it openly known that he had given up drinking entirely to observe the Prohibition laws and no longer served liquor in the White House.

Hard Work and Long Hours

Harding certainly enjoyed golf, poker, and the company of his close friends. He did not possess Wilson's intellect or his knowledge of history, economics, and law. Nor did he bring to the presidency Roosevelt's ambition and drive. However, Harding was a very hardworking President and did not try to shirk or avoid the grueling duties of his office.

According to many who observed him in the White House, Harding worked harder at the job than either Wilson or Roosevelt and did double the work of Taft. Ike Hoover, who had served as head usher in the White House for 42 years, said that Harding was one of the hardest-working Presidents he had ever known. Hoover also pointed out that even when Harding was engaged in golfing, traveling, or meals, he was "working" and using the time to discuss official business.

Like many Presidents, it was said that Harding grew into his role as chief executive and took his job more seriously every day. His perspective on the presidency was much different after only a short time in office than it had been while he sat in the Senate or even when he campaigned. As his months in office passed, his idea of what it meant to be President would change even more.

Chapter **8**

A Rocky Road to "Normalcy"

W hen Harding took office in 1921, his administration faced many postwar problems. The two major problems that demanded his immediate attention were revising the tax system and passing an emergency tariff law to help farmers.

TACKLING THE ISSUES

A special session of Congress was convened on April 11. Harding addressed the assembly the next day, calling for a cutback of government spending and approval of a national budget system. He also asked Congress to lower certain taxes, repeal other taxes, enact tariff legislation, lower railroad rates, and promote agricultural interests. He spoke about two special projects in which he was particularly interested, building up the merchant marine and the creation of a Department of Public Welfare to oversee such matters as education, health, and the building of highways.

Since Wilson's Versailles Treaty had never been ratified by the Senate because of the disagreement over the League of Nations issue, the United States was technically still at war with Germany. Harding now asked Congress "to establish a state of technical peace without further delay." On July 2, 1921, he signed the Knox-Porter Resolution (which included many of the provisions contained in the Versailles Treaty, though the United States never ratified it), thereby finally ending the war.

Lack of Decisive Leadership

On the basis of his address to the special session of Congress, it was apparent that Harding would not be as pliable a President as some had expected. However, in the months that followed, he did not guide Congress with a strong hand. Harding believed that the President should deliver his agenda and then leave it to Congress to work out the necessary legislation. The presidency, he thought, should be above the partisan infighting of Congress.

Furthermore, Harding's way had always been to gather many thoughts and points of view on a question and then arrive at an answer that was a consensus of opinion. He believed in calling in experts or "the best minds" on any given topic, which is how he chose the members of his Cabinet.

It was a problem-solving method that had worked for Harding so far. But now as President, this method did not serve either him or the country very well. He would listen to one side of an argument and see its logic, then listen to another side and be equally convinced.

Harding had asked Congress to address the tax and tariff problems first. But despite his best intentions, the legislative branch made little progress in the first months of his administration, partly because he lacked decisive presidential leadership. Also, the Republican majority, which Harding had thought would cooperate with him, split into various special-interest blocs in both the House of Representatives and the Senate.

THE PLIGHT OF THE FARMERS

At the start of the special congressional session, Senator Robert La Follette of Wisconsin organized a group of 27 senators into a farm bloc to fight for the needs of the farmers whom they represented. These senators felt that Harding's policies were quickly shaping up to favor business and the eastern banking establishments. They wanted the government to help relieve the farmers' financial crisis.

Two weeks after Harding's address to Congress, the National Farmers' Union sent the President a statement, describing their difficulties:

> The farmers are overwhelmed with debt. They are unable to buy necessary fertilizer. They cannot obtain needed credit and there are in hundreds and thousands of cases no markets open to them . . . they are the innocent victims of a misused economic system, manipulated, we fear, by shortsighted and selfish interests.

The statement went on to refer to the President and to the priorities of his administration. The union was particularly concerned about Secretary of the Treasury Andrew Mellon, one of the richest men in America, who was about to revise the nation's tax system:

> Some citizens, who have not felt the sting of adversity, are insisting that things are all right and they will correct themselves. They are living in . . . great wealth and are wondering why anybody should complain. They know nothing that should be reformed except the income tax schedule and this they think should be scaled down.

No Government Aid

Harding's reaction to the union statement was not a very sympathetic one, nor did he change his view of the problems. He stuck to the "boom and bust" theory, or an "ebb and flow" notion of economics. Depression would always follow a period of inflation or a "boom," like the wartime economic spurt. The economy would correct itself eventually, just as high tide eventually follows low.

Harding maintained that Americans had to be patient and wait out the depression. Any government interference in the regular economic cycle might help temporarily but could foul up the system in the long run. Assistance to the unemployed was the responsibility of local governments, he affirmed. He did not favor federal aid or "paternalism" to either agriculture or industry. "The farmer requires no special favors at the hands of government," Harding said. "All he needs is a fair chance."

Harding's reply enraged the farm bloc senators. Senator George Norris of Nebraska, chairman of the Senate Committee on Agriculture and a leader of the bloc, quickly introduced a bill to create a Farmer's Export Financing Corporation, which Norris believed would help agricultural export. The bill was complicated and designed to address the double problem of giving food relief to Europe and ending the farm surpluses at home. The bill called for the government to establish a corporation to buy farm surpluses for cash and then sell them abroad for credit for a five-year period.

Two members of Harding's Cabinet, Mellon and Secretary of Commerce Herbert Hoover, opposed the Norris bill. Harding was aware that farmers had suffered a disastrous slump in the price of farm products. However, his position was that the farmers were not the only ones affected by the price slump, nor did bankers exploit them.

Some Help from Congress

Although the Norris bill was not passed, an alternative plan giving farmers a billion dollars worth of loans through the War Finance Corporation was passed. Called the Emergency Agricultural Credit Act, it was signed on August 24, 1921, after having originated in the White House, not Congress.

According to this act, the War Finance Corporation was authorized to loan money to farmers' cooperatives and foreign purchasers. It was also authorized to grant loans for the breeding, raising, and marketing of livestock, and to give aid to badly depressed banks in agricultural areas of the country. By 1923 the War Finance Corporation had loaned about $420 million under this act.

More help for the farmer during Harding's administration included a restriction on speculation in wheat and regulation of the packing and stockyard industry. An Emergency Tariff Bill was eventually passed that raised tariffs on agricultural products coming into the country so that they would be more expensive than American farm products. But it was only a temporary measure until a more permanent law was worked out in Congress.

On August 19, 1922, the Senate finally enacted a permanent tariff law. The act gave the President the right to raise or lower tariff rates up to a certain amount. At last, it seemed like American farmers and businessmen had adequate protection in the marketplace against foreign imports.

The tariff act passed in 1922 established the highest tariff rates in the history of the country and gave some temporary relief to industry and farming. Farmers soon discovered, however, that the dollars they gained in the marketplace had to be used to pay the increased cost on certain manufactured goods. In the long run, the law resulted in disastrous problems for the United States by isolating the country economically from the rest of the world.

MONEY, MONEY, MONEY

One of the foremost achievements of Harding's administration was the creation of a national budget system. Harding was dedicated to cutting waste in federal spending and reducing the national debt.

Up until this time, there had been no overall plan or control of the government's expenditures. There was no central office or bureau that watched over and investigated the money spent by the many departments in the federal government. Every December, Congress would receive budget requests from each department detailing how much money was needed to run the department for the coming year. These requests were compiled and passed on to Congress by the Treasury Department, which did not check to see if the requests were valid or accurate. This system was both inefficient and time consuming. Moreover, it also failed to give a clear picture of how much the government was spending and where the money was going.

A bill for a national budget system had been introduced during the Wilson administration. However, Wilson did not approve the bill because it gave the secretary of the treasury, not the President, direct responsibility for the federal budget. Harding, on the other hand, was able to get a budget bill through Congress that put control of the nation's pocketbook in the President's hands.

The Budget and Accounting Act of 1921 was signed by Harding on June 10. The President would appoint a director and an assistant director of the Budget Bureau. The act required that the President, with the aid of the Budget Bureau, would draw up an annual budget that would be presented to Congress. The budget would include complete information regarding revenues, expenses, the condition of the national treasury, and a forecast of the administration's plans for future spending.

Trimming the Fat

Harding thought that his choice of a director for the Budget Bureau would be the most important appointment he would ever have to make. He knew exactly who he wanted – Charles Dawes. Harding had asked Dawes to join his Cabinet as secretary of the treasury, but Dawes had refused the post.

Dawes had served President McKinley as comptroller of the treasury and had risen to the rank of general during the war, when he was in charge of procuring Army supplies. He had a reputation for efficiency and blunt speech that often offended people. He could be charming one minute and curt the next. His public speeches were sometimes likened to the fire-and-brimstone sermons of Bible-thumping preachers. He was known to interrupt flattery by saying, "Cut out all the flub dubs." Dawes took the job knowing that it would be a difficult one – like using a "toothpick . . . to tunnel Pike's Peak" he told the President.

Harding promised Dawes that he would have his complete support and that "the Bureau of the Budget shall be impersonal, impartial, and non-political." Dawes began his new post by addressing the first meeting of the Business Organization of the Government, a group that included members of the Cabinet and 1,200 bureau chiefs. The goal of the Budget Bureau, he told them, was to trim the "fat" from requests and eliminate extravagance.

Despite resistance from Harding's Cabinet and various bureau heads, Dawes and Harding were successful in establishing the first coordinated budget in the nation's history. On December 5, 1921, Harding presented this budget to Congress. He and Dawes were afraid that Congress would nitpick and tear the budget to shreds. But after a few minor alterations, the budget was passed easily. Both the Congress and the American people were pleased by the new orderly system of business management applied to the government. It was felt to be a very positive sign towards the nation's overall economic recovery.

Under Dawes' direction and Harding's firm support, the government reduced spending by almost $1.4 billion in the fiscal year ending June 30, 1922. By the end of the next year, federal expenses were cut about $500 million more and were almost $2 billion less than in 1921, the final year of Wilson's administration.

REVISING THE TAX SYSTEM

During Wilson's years, taxes on businesses and individuals had been raised to pay the high cost of America's entry into World War I. When Harding took office, the nation was clamoring for taxes to be lowered from the high wartime rates and wanted a complete revision of the tax structure.

Harding was determined to fulfill his campaign promise of lowering taxes. However, his appointment of Andrew Mellon as secretary of the treasury had a great effect on the way in which this promise was met.

A Man of Great Wealth

Andrew Mellon was one of the richest men in the United States. He was the son of a wealthy Pittsburgh banker and used the family fortune to build the Mellon Bank. His wealth was not derived from a single product or activity (like Henry Ford, for instance, who had made his fortune by manufacturing cars). Mellon was a finance capitalist. He invested his money in a vast array of industries: steel, railroads, public utilities, water power, distilleries, insurance firms, coal, aluminum, and oil. His fortune grew when these investments earned a profit.

Until he was appointed to Harding's Cabinet, Mellon had little involvement in politics. He also knew little about the Treasury Department and its history, or about advanced economic theory or international loans and trade. However, Mellon had firsthand experience in high finance with fantastic success. Selecting Mellon as secretary of the treasury pleased the business and banking community. They believed that Harding's administration would be on their side. But agriculture and labor were unhappy about Mellon's appointment because they also assumed that he would favor business.

Mellon was not well liked. Slight and frail-looking, he always wore dark clothes with a black tie, drooping black socks, and a buttoned coat. He was very quiet, even in Cabinet meetings. Once Harding referred to him as "the Sphinx." He rarely smiled and only shook hands with the tips of his fingers. His personality was the complete opposite of Harding. Some believed that Mellon had great influence over Harding, but there is little evidence in their personal correspondence to support this assumption. Harding respected Mellon's opinion but did not rely upon Mellon as a confidential advisor.

Mellon believed that three steps were necessary to restore prosperity: decreasing taxes, reducing the national debt, and cutting back government spending. Dawes had taken care of the last item. Most everyone agreed an immediate change in the tax structure was necessary. However, Mellon's view of the problem strongly favored the wealthy and upper middle-income groups and gave little relief to the poor.

A Rich Man's Bias

With economic views that showed the bias of a millionaire, Mellon did not see taxes as a way to fight social problems or redistribute the nation's wealth. Rather, he believed that the goal of taxation was to "bring in a maximum amount of revenue to the Treasury and at the same time bear not too heavily on the taxpayer or on business enterprises."

Mellon thought that the use of an income tax and the demands of financing the war had put the larger burden of taxes on the wealthy and upper middle-income groups. He thought that high taxation did not bring in more revenue for the government or redistribute wealth. He believed that the rich simply avoided paying the correct amount of taxes on their real income by placing a large portion of their money into nontaxable areas, such as tax-exempt securities.

If tax rates were decreased for the rich, Mellon argued, the government had a better chance of collecting more taxes and also boosting business and industry. The rich and upper middle class, Mellon said, would use their extra income to invest in business and promote economic growth. In order to bring about economic recovery, he believed, relief from high taxes had to be given to this group.

Under the Revenue Act of 1918, amended in 1919, the tax rates for individuals were four percent on the first $4,000 of income and eight percent on any income above that level. Surtax rates (taxes over and above regular taxes) increased from one percent on incomes greater than $5,000 to a maximum of 65 percent on incomes over one million dollars. Corporations were taxed 10 percent, and an excess-profits tax was also levied on profits over a certain amount. When Mellon appeared before the House Ways and Means Committee, he recommended that the surtax on large incomes be cut in half, from 65 percent to 32 percent. He also suggested that the general income tax rates of four percent and eight percent remain the same.

Harding's "Tax Melon"

There was great objection to Mellon's plan. Opponents in the House of Representatives called it a rich man's measure; the newspapers called it the administration's "tax melon." Farm and labor groups claimed the bill was a gift to corporations and were outraged at the idea of lower taxes for the rich while many laborers were out of work and many farmers were on the verge of losing their farms.

President Harding was torn. The tax problem was a complicated issue that he did not fully understand. He would listen to the arguments on each side and see merit in all of them. As usual, he sought to compromise and find a middle ground on the differences. Because he had respect for Mellon's financial knowledge, he supported Mellon's plan without fully understanding it or the arguments against it.

When Mellon's tax plan reached the Senate, a bill for giving veterans added compensation (a "bonus") for having served in the war was under consideration. Harding expressed deep sympathy with the veterans but was strongly opposed to the bill, which would cost the government many millions of dollars. He felt the expense would undermine the efforts of both Dawes and Mellon to stabilize the economy.

Taking an Unpopular Stand

Harding appeared before the Senate on July 12, 1921, urging that the tax revision bill be passed immediately. He warned that passing the soldiers' bonus bill at this time would be "a disaster to the nation's finances." Despite predictions that opposing the soldiers' bonus bill would be an unpopular stand, Harding was praised by the public and newspapers for his position. *The New York Times* said his forceful stand on the issue was one of a "President of the whole people, not an opportunist politician."

Congress heeded the popular President's warning and did not pass the bonus bill at that time. However, they did not iron out a final tax plan until months later. The Revenue Act of 1921 was passed on November 23, the last day of Congress' special session. It was a compromise between Mellon's plan and the demands of his opponents. The repeal of excess-profits tax was scheduled for January 1, 1922. For the very wealthy, the maximum surtax rate was changed from 65 percent to 50 percent, not 32 percent as Mellon had wanted.

Also, individuals with lower incomes were given more exemptions (tax benefits) than Mellon had suggested.

Overall, the tax revision was not a drastic change from the past and did not greatly change the situation of either the wealthy or the poor. However, Harding had lowered taxes, as he had promised. Together with the cutbacks in government spending, the tax reductions did give some needed boost to business and pushed along economic recovery.

STAND ON CIVIL RIGHTS

During the summer of his first year in office, Harding took time out from his battles with Congress to visit Birmingham, Alabama, for the celebration of the city's 50th anniversary. Speaking at Capitol Park to a group of about 20,000 whites and 10,000 blacks, Harding's speech shocked many when he bluntly pointed out that America would not be a true democracy until blacks had obtained political and economic equality.

It was a surprising and bold stand. The blacks in the audience cheered Harding while the whites sat in stunned, stony silence. The speech marked Harding as a leading advocate for civil rights in his party and among post-Civil War Presidents. The address was even more impressive because it was delivered in the South, the stronghold of race prejudice, discrimination, and the Ku Klux Klan (a white hate group dedicated to racial prejudice).

Political, economic, and educational equality for blacks would benefit not only American democracy but the South as well, Harding said. By modern standards, his civil rights views (which accepted social and educational segregation) were not a vision of total, uncompromised equality. However, at the time, his stand on civil rights was extremely liberal, certainly far more liberal than Woodrow Wilson's. The speech drew as much praise as it did criticism.

A CONFERENCE ON DISARMAMENT

While the special session of Congress was tied in knots over domestic issues, Harding set out on a dramatic effort at foreign relations. Working with Secretary of State Charles Evans Hughes, Harding invited leaders from England and Japan to Washington, D.C., in order to discuss a reduction in arms, particularly naval armaments. Since World War I, America had been competing with other world powers in a race to build a superior navy.

But after the war, support for a policy of disarmament was growing in both Houses of Congress. Continuing to pour money into building military weapons was also not in keeping with current trends towards peace and economy.

The Washington Conference on Disarmament opened dramatically on Armistice Day, November 11, 1921. Coincidentally, but quite fittingly, the day had been chosen for the dedication of the Tomb of the Unknown Soldier. A solemn and impressive procession began at the Capitol and ended at Arlington National Cemetery, where the Tomb was located. Both Harding and Wilson took part in the ceremonies.

At the graveside, Harding addressed an audience of about 100,000, which included foreign dignitaries who had arrived for the conference. He said, "There must, there shall be, the commanding voice of a conscious civilization against armed warfare."

Scrapping the World's Warships

The conference began the next day. Secretary Hughes shocked the group with his opening statement, a plan for each of the superpowers to scrap a total of 1,878,043 tons of their warships. According to Hughes' proposal, the United States would be left with 500,650 tons, Great Britain with 604,450, and Japan with 299,700. There were also limits set for the French and Italian navies. He further suggested a 10-year halt in new construction with limits for replacement.

Several treaties emerged from the conference. One abolished the use of poisonous gas and submarines. Another had to do with foreign relations in the Pacific. The most famous of the treaties, the Five-Power Naval Treaty, emerged from Secretary Hughes' proposal for reducing the size of the world's great navies and thereby limiting any nation's ability to wage war.

Harding asked the Senate to approve the treaties on February 10, 1922, because he believed that they were "absolutely essential to the welfare of the United States." Although the treaties met some opposition in Congress, the press and public were greatly in favor of Harding's efforts to secure world peace. The Senate finally ratified the treaties on April 1.

At the time, the press, public, and politicians believed that the Washington Conference on Disarmament (and the treaties that had been negotiated there) would establish a place of honor for President Harding in the pages of history. The meeting's successful outcome certainly brightened the nation's outlook on the future. In retrospect, however, the treaties have been criticized for naively clearing the way for subsequent Japanese expansion.

The treaties were among many efforts to ensure international peace in the years between World War I and World War II. But contrary to the impression that prevailed in the spring of 1922, Harding and his administration would not be remembered for the Washington Conference on Disarmament, but for the scandals and disgrace yet to come.

AMNESTY FOR WAR PROTESTORS

Harding ended the year 1921 with a well-publicized humanitarian act, granting amnesty (pardons) to many war protestors who had been in jail for the past three years. Among

The Washington Conference on Disarmament opened on November 11, 1921. Several treaties emerged from the conference. One served to limit the size of the world's great navies and thereby reduce the ability of the superpowers to wage war. (Library of Congress.)

these was Eugene V. Debs, a leader of the Socialist Party who had been nominated to run for President in 1920 while serving a jail term in the Atlanta State Penitentiary. The 65-year-old Debs had been arrested in the summer of 1918 for antiwar activity.

As soon as Harding was elected, he had been urged to release wartime political prisoners, particularly Debs. There were also, however, angry voices in the press and Congress which were opposed to amnesty for political prisoners. Nevertheless, Harding had Attorney General Daugherty investigate the matter and interview Debs in Atlanta.

Home for Christmas

Under Harding's approval, Debs and 23 other political prisoners were released on December 24, 1921. Daugherty had suggested New Year's Eve as a release date, but Harding said he wanted Debs to get home in time to "eat Christmas dinner with his wife." Debs did not know he was going to be freed until the day he was released. Tears streamed down his eyes as over 2,000 of his fellow inmates cheered his departure.

Harding had requested that the labor leader and social activist stop off in Washington, D.C., on his way home to Indiana. Debs and Harding met privately in the President's office. When Debs came out of the meeting and was greeted by reporters, he seemed to have been impressed by the President. "Mr. Harding appears to me to be a kind gentleman, one who I believe possesses humane impulses." Debs continued on his way to Terre Haute, Indiana, for his Christmas dinner, which was delayed by two days.

Harding was harshly criticized by many for releasing Debs. But his tough choice came from his heart and moral conscience, not a wish to take whatever stand would boost his own popularity. Harding wrote to a friend, "I was persuaded in my own mind that it was the right thing to do. . . . I thought the spirit of clemency was quite in harmony with the things we were trying to do here in Washington."

Instead of granting general amnesty for political prisoners, as many countries had done after the war, Harding reviewed each case individually. He was criticized by some for this slow process of personal review. He granted a release on the basis of whether the person had committed any criminal or destructive act in connection with his antiwar protests. He had reviewed and released most of the wartime prisoners by the time of his death in 1923.

Chapter 9

Labor Strikes Back

T he most urgent problems Harding faced during the second year of his presidency had to do with the conflict between labor and management. When he took office during the uneasy postwar period, there was a series of strikes in many industries: shipping, printing, textile, and meat-packing, to name but a few. The workers wanted an eight-hour workday, a shorter workweek, better working conditions, and higher wages.

Harding tried to keep the government out of the disputes between labor and management. At first, he did not interfere, except in the shipping strike, which affected government-owned ships. His policy was that government should not take sides between business and labor but should work behind the scenes to help both sides find solutions and settle their differences. Harding's hands-off policies were to be tested, however, first by his quest to end the 12-hour workday and also by the railroad and coal miners' strikes.

SHORTENING THE WORKDAY

Influenced by Secretary of Commerce Herbert Hoover, Harding tried hard to persuade the men who ran the steel and iron industry to abolish the 12-hour workday. There had been a large, violent strike of steel workers in 1919, and it was feared that there might be another if the difficult, inhumane working conditions were not changed. One of these was the out-moded and grueling 12-hour day.

In the spring of 1922, the President invited a group of 41 top executives in the steel industry to the White House to discuss the issue. Headed by Elbert Gary, the chief of United States Steel, the only promise the captains of industry would grant the President was to study the matter further.

After a year of study, the President's request was rejected. Management of the steel and iron industry argued that cutting back to an eight-hour workday would raise the cost of making steel by 15 percent and would require 60,000 more workers. They did not feel, as Harding did, that the 12-hour day was old-fashioned or harmful in any way to their employees.

Winning the Battle

There was a great public outcry against the steel industry's position. Harding was very distressed and would not accept the refusal of his request. Secretary of Labor James Davis and Hoover drafted a strong letter that sharply criticized the steelmen's position. It was usually Harding's way to tactfully and gently persuade those who disagreed with him. But this time, he made no effort to soften the blunt language of Hoover and Davis' letter. With Harding's signature on the bottom, the letter was sent to Elbert Gary on June 18, 1923.

A week later, President Harding received a reply by telegram while traveling through the Pacific Northwest on his way to Alaska. The men who ran the steel industry would finally bend to popular opinion and Harding's wishes. This time they told the President that they would "exert every effort at our command to secure in the iron and steel industry of this country a total abolition of the 12-hour day at the earliest time practicable."

Winning this battle with the steel industry was a proud

moment for Harding. He believed that the goodwill shown by the steel industry would heal some rifts between management and labor, and also improve the quality of American life. Fatefully enough, United States Steel announced that the eight-hour day would begin at once in their mills on August 2, the day Harding died.

RAILROAD AND MINING STRIKES

Harding approved of unions in principle and respected the legal rights of workers to organize and strike. But on the other hand, he did not believe that unions should dictate to government. He did not deny management the power to break strikes by use of the open shop (employing nonunion workers) and scab labor, or strikebreakers. He supported the general principle of the open shop and took the position that "every American citizen, whether union or nonunion, should have the privilege of working where and when he pleases and should be guaranteed protection by the government in the exercise of this right as an American citizen."

Harding believed that employers had a moral responsibility to treat their employees in a benevolent, almost paternalistic manner, just as he had treated his employees at the *Star*. When disagreements erupted, he thought discussion, compromise, and conciliation were the best means to resolving problems. He considered strikes a last resort, a choice that left scars and caused hardship for both sides and for the American public.

In January 1922, textile workers in New England went out on strike in protest of reduced wages and an increased workweek. The strike involved over 100,000 workers and lasted six months, but the workers finally won.

Soon after the textile strike, John L. Lewis, head of the United Mine Workers, organized a strike of over 650,000 coal miners. The strike was called in opposition to wage cuts and the introduction of an irregular workweek. But before Harding's administration had time to react to the coal miners' strike, more trouble arose in the rail yards. On July 1, almost 400,000 members of the Railway Shopmen Union walked off their jobs. Again, according to the government's Railroad Labor Board, the primary issue was wage reductions.

At first Harding's approach was to watch, wait, and encourage conciliation, but avoid interfering in the disputes. Meanwhile, the disruption of the railroads caused problems for businesses and farmers trying to transport their goods. And as the nation's coal supplies dwindled, people began to wonder what would happen with winter approaching.

It was while these two strikes were going on that the President was trying to persuade the steel industry to abolish the 12-hour workday. Although the effort would benefit the workman's cause in general, it did not do much to settle the ongoing disputes.

Bloodshed in the Coal Fields

In late June, the coal strike erupted with violence and bloodshed as armed miners killed 20 strikebreakers who were trying to reopen a mine in Herrin, Illinois. Pressure on the government to settle the strike was now overwhelming. President Harding's hands-off policy would no longer do.

Harding called John L. Lewis and the mine owners to a conference in the White House. Secretary of Labor Davis presented both sides with a presidential proposal to settle the strike. However, even with the guidance of the government, labor and the coal operators could not arrive at an agreement. Harding was thoroughly frustrated and saw further attempts at mediating to be useless. He told mine owners to resume operation as best as possible, pledging that the government—on the state and federal level—would ensure conditions for the production of coal and "lawful operations."

The President's efforts to settle the railroad strike met

with the same frustrating results. Together with Davis and Hoover, Harding outlined a three-point mediation proposal. The union accepted the plan, but railroad executives rejected a provision which asked that all employees on strike be returned to their former positions with seniority and other rights unimpaired.

Harding made one last attempt to bring the carriers and workers together in early August. But this effort failed, too. The man who had been known during his years in the Senate as the Great Harmonizer now could not settle either of the two labor-management disputes despite his best efforts at compromise and persuasion. Taking this failure personally, he felt frustrated and betrayed by both labor and management.

Appeals to Congress

On August 18, President Harding turned to Congress for help in settling the mining and railroad strikes. In an address to Congress, he took note of the increasing violence on railroad lines and sent a strong message to labor that the government would no longer sit on its hands when laws were being broken:

> There are statutes forbidding conspiracy to hinder interstate commerce. There are laws to assure the highest possible safety in railway service. It is my purpose to invoke these laws, civil and criminal, against all offenders alike.

At the same time, Harding also reminded management that labor unions were recognized by law, and the government had "no sympathy or approval" for "warfare" on the unions.

Congress quickly passed a bill to study the coal industry and make recommendations. Another bill was also passed before the end of the month that contained the administration's plan for the pricing, control, and distribution of coal during the strike emergency. In other words, if a shortage of coal due to the strike created a national emergency, the government would be sanctioned by law to take control of the mines.

These congressional acts pushed the miners and mine owners closer towards a settlement. The union was afraid that if the strike was not settled by the winter, the government would make good on its threat to take over the mines. The two sides met again in Washington, D.C., on August 29. At first, they could not settle. But just at this time, dramatic events involving government action ended the railroad strike on September 1. Not surprisingly, the miners' union and mine owners were able to come to an agreement a few days later.

The Wilkerson Injunction

The railroad strike came to an abrupt end shortly before the coal miners settled. However, the form of government intervention used to end the walkout forever branded Harding as a hard-nosed, antilabor President who was willing to trample civil rights in order to break a strike. Although a strong case could be made for his sympathy towards business, Harding had maintained a hands-off policy in both strikes as long as he possibly could. And even when he did step into the disputes, he respected the legal rights of the unions.

Attorney General Daugherty, however, had always pushed the President to use tougher legal action against the strikers. In Cabinet meetings, he argued with Harding, Hoover, and Davis, of all whom favored mediation and a mild approach. Daugherty believed that the strikes were inspired by "Reds" and "bolshevism." He tried to persuade others, Harding included, that the strikes were a warning sign of an impending revolution. Daugherty was alone in his belief. Others in the Cabinet wanted Harding to take stronger antilabor action, but for economic reasons.

Disregarding Constitutional Rights

On September 1, Daugherty went to Chicago and appeared before Judge James H. Wilkerson. He petitioned the court for a broad and severe restraining order against the rail strikers. The injunction Wilkerson issued was the most sweeping in American labor history. It was also unconstitutional and denied strikers their rights under the law.

The Wilkerson injunction forbid strikers to interfere in any way with strikebreaking on the railroads. They could not even picket peacefully or incite others to picket. They could not issue strike directions or encourage the strike by letters, telegrams, telephones, or word of mouth, nor could they use union funds to continue the strike. By a blatant disregard for constitutional rights, the strike was broken in two days.

It is not completely clear if Harding knew of Daugherty's strike-breaking plan. Telegrams found in his papers suggest that the President did know where Daugherty was and what he planned to do. When Daugherty returned to Washington and met with the Cabinet and President, he was blasted on all sides for his action, particularly by Hoover and Secretary of State Charles Evans Hughes, who called the injunction "outrageous in law as well as morals." It was obvious that even if Harding had secretly approved of Daugherty's action, he had not understood the sweeping implications of the injunction and the violation of the strikers' civil rights.

Once Harding fully understood what had happened, he turned on Daugherty with such anger, Hoover reported, that Daugherty "was flabbergasted." Harding ordered Daugherty to withdraw the objectionable sections of the injunction immediately. The President quickly announced to the public that the administration's purpose was not to violate civil liberties, but to prevent interference with interstate commerce and protect the safety of the public.

Labor leaders across the country were outraged. They demanded that Daugherty be removed from office, and Harding could have insisted that Daugherty resign. But for reasons still unknown, he remained loyal to Daugherty, who was already under fire from certain members of Congress for growing scandals in the Justice Department.

Chapter 10

The Beginning of an Unhappy End

As 1923 began, trouble was brewing in the Harding administration. Everywhere the President turned, there were rumors of scandals and abuses of power by men whom he had personally appointed. Some were even trusted friends, like Albert Fall, Harry Daugherty, and Charles Forbes.

THE TEAPOT DOME SPILLS OVER

In January 1923, Harding accepted the resignation of Albert Fall, secretary of the interior. Since the spring of 1922, Fall's activities had been under Senate investigation.

Formerly a senator from New Mexico, Fall became friendly with Harding while both were serving in the Senate. Fall's appointment to Harding's Cabinet was not generally commented upon, and many regarded him as hardworking and efficient. He was criticized, however, by dedicated conservationists like Gifford Pinchot, the commissioner of forestry in Pennsylvania, and Henry A. Slattery, the secretary of the National Conservation Association. They knew that Fall did not agree with the existing policy of preserving and protecting natural resources and were suspicious of him from the start.

Under Presidents Taft and Wilson, certain tracts of land out West that contained great oil reserves had been set aside for the future needs of the U.S. Navy. Suspicions about Fall were further aroused when he persuaded Harding in 1921 to transfer the control of these oil reserves to his jurisdiction, the Department of the Interior. Conservationists suspected even then that Fall had plans for making some personal profit from these rich oil reserves.

Leasing of government-owned oil lands was not illegal as it had been authorized by Congress. The Navy might possibly need the oil in the event of another war, but first it had to be extracted. Private companies had to be hired to drill and store it. Accordingly, a private lease to drill on a federal oil reserve located in California was granted to Edward Doheny on July 12, 1921. Doheny was chosen through open, competitive bidding—a system that awarded the job to the oil company that promised to do it for the least amount of money.

Harding was in favor of conservation, but he also believed in a limited development of natural resources.

Secret Leases

However, by the following spring, there were rumors that more leases had been granted secretly in California and in a reserve near Salt Creek, Wyoming, known as Teapot Dome. The Teapot Dome reserve had been leased on April 7, 1922, to Harry Sinclair's Mammoth Oil Company.

After conservationists found out about the leases a few days later, Senator John Kendrick of Wyoming demanded that Fall come forward with information about the leases. Fall admitted to leasing the Teapot Dome reserve to Sinclair and to granting another lease to Doheny on the California reserve.

In exchange for the leases, the government was to receive a percentage of the profits, as well as storage tanks and pipelines to be built on the West Coast and at Pearl Harbor.

Fall had been secretary of the interior for a little more than a year, and in that relatively short period of time, he managed to lease out three naval oil reserves to Sinclair and Doheny for a percentage payable to the government. When Fall claimed he did not open the leases up to competitive bidding because national security was involved, his explanation was not accepted by Congress. On April 28, 1922, the Senate proposed to investigate the oil lease situation.

The wheels of the Senate committee moved slowly. There was almost a truckload of documents to sift through and examine. While the investigation moved along at a snail's pace, the newspapers gave the story little attention. The coal and railroad strikes were the big news that spring. The story would not be carried by the press until after the President's death.

Harding stood by Fall and doggedly maintained a belief in Fall's integrity. Fall resigned his Cabinet post in January 1923 in order to pursue private business interests. Not surprisingly, he took a job with Sinclair's oil company.

THE WAY THE WIND BLOWS

Attorney General Harry Daugherty had once remarked about political life, "If a man in politics complains about the way the wind blows, he had better stay out of politics and out of the wind." After the Wilkerson injunction, a hard wind from Congress nearly blew Daugherty off Capitol Hill.

Even before the Wilkerson injunction, certain members of Congress had tried to discredit Daugherty, claiming that he was abusing the powers of his office. Now they believed they had ample ammunition to either impeach him or force him to resign.

On December 1, 1922, Representative Oscar Keller of Minnesota filed 14 charges of impeachment against Daugherty before the House Committee on the Judiciary. Violating constitutional rights of citizens, failing to enforce antitrust laws, undermining the Federal Trade Commission, and using his office in the Justice Department for personal gain were among Keller's serious claims.

A Senate investigation into the impeachment charges began 10 days later, but it took only two days to hear all the testimony. Although Keller's charges were strong, he had not assembled enough evidence to prove Daugherty guilty of any specific act. Daugherty defended himself vigorously, hinting that this attempt to impeach him was obviously masterminded by "radical" forces of "Reds." Daugherty was cleared of all charges. The hearing resulted, not in Daugherty's public disgrace, but in Keller's.

Two Old Cronies

Although Daugherty might have called on the President for help, he faced the impeachment committee alone and held his ground. If Harding believed any part of the charges against Daugherty, he kept his suspicions to himself. Publicly he stood by Daugherty, as he had stood by Fall. When asked, Harding denied that he had any intention of asking Daugherty to resign. Many considered the attack on Daugherty nothing more than an act of revenge by prolabor groups for the Wilkerson injunction. Harding tended to agree.

The President and Daugherty first became acquainted through Ohio politics. Daugherty, an attorney, had served in the state legislature and had worked as a lobbyist (one who tries to influence public officials on legislation) in Columbus. He supported Harding's run for the U.S. Senate in 1914, and their relationship became much closer when Daugherty ran his presidential campaign.

When Harding appointed Daugherty to his Cabinet as attorney general, he was criticized for the choice because of Daugherty's lack of qualifications for the job and his questionable integrity as a former lobbyist. However, his Cabinet appointments seemed generally sound to both the press and Senate. If some senators had planned to fight Daugherty's appointment, they were caught off guard.

Although he publicly stood by Daugherty during the impeachment proceedings, some sources say that the President was privately disillusioned and disappointed by the events. He was drawing away from his old Ohio friend at this time and turning more toward men like Hoover, Hughes, and Mellon for advice.

RUMORS, RUMORS EVERYWHERE

Rumors of more wrong-doings on Capitol Hill persisted, involving Daugherty, Fall, and others close to the President. Many of these men were minor appointees who were Daugherty's friends from Ohio. This group became known as the Ohio Gang, a group with which the President was acquainted but not on close personal terms. However, after Harding's death, rumors were circulated that the President had more to do with this group of lobbyists and profiteers than was actually true.

The President at first brushed aside talk of corruption in his administration. It was only malicious gossip, he thought, spun out at a wholesale rate by his enemies in Congress. Particularly to blame was the prolabor faction, which had gone after Daugherty. They were eager to discredit his administration and ruin his chances for a second term. Harding was sure if he simply ignored all the talk, it would die down.

Mrs. Harding, however, was not so sure. She urged her husband to be less trusting of his "friends." Florence believed in astrology and consulted a clairvoyant named Madame Marcia who lived in Washington. Casting Harding's horoscope in 1920, it is reported that Madame Marcia predicted that if Harding ran for President, he would definitely be elected; but, she added, he would die in office.

It is not known how often Florence Harding consulted Madame Marcia for advice, but a note found in her household account book pertaining to the early months of 1923 had some astrological advice for Harding: "His horoscope shows he cannot depend upon his friends. He would be suspicious of the ones he should trust and [would] trust those he should be suspicious of."

Another Rotten Apple

Like Albert Fall, Charles Forbes was another trusted friend of whom Harding should have been suspicious. They had met in Hawaii when Forbes was in charge of building the Pearl Harbor naval base in 1915. Forbes had a distinguished war record and won the Congressional Medal of Honor during World War I. However, earlier records show he had once deserted the Army and was arrested, though never brought to trial.

Charlie Forbes was personable and charming; he enjoyed parties and card playing. He was a favorite guest of both the President and the First Lady. When Harding appointed Forbes director of the Veterans' Bureau, he was warned, even by Daugherty, that Forbes was not entirely trustworthy.

But if Harding had one great flaw, it was his inability to see the shortcomings of people he liked. This blind spot eventually proved to be his undoing. He gave Forbes the post and was proud of the work Forbes did from 1920 to 1922, building hospitals around the country for veterans.

In the late months of 1922, rumors abounded that Forbes

was using his position to carry on illegal profiteering schemes. When called to the White House for an explanation, Forbes convinced the President that there was no need for concern.

In mid-February of 1923 (shortly after Fall's resignation and Daugherty's investigation by the Senate), Harding was presented with conclusive evidence of Forbes' illegal activities. Forbes had been selling government medical supplies to private contractors and pocketing the proceeds. He was also collecting graft and bribes related to hospital building contracts and site selection.

President Harding was shocked and angry. He had always revered the quality of loyalty, and betrayal from a trusted friend was a hard blow. He called Forbes to the White House again. According to one report, at this meeting the President nearly choked Forbes, calling him a double-crosser. He demanded Forbes' resignation. Forbes quickly left the country, and his resignation was sent to Washington from Europe on February 15.

Harding could have taken more severe action against Forbes; he could have exposed his crimes and brought legal charges against him. He could have also asked Congress to investigate the situation. It is impossible to say why he did not take such steps. Perhaps he believed that Forbes' illegal activities would remain hidden and it was enough simply to remove him from office. Or maybe it was difficult for him to admit publicly that he had been so wrong in judging Forbes' character.

The President may have even been afraid that revealing the Forbes situation to the public would cast a dark shadow over his entire administration. It would provide his opponents in Congress with plenty more ammunition to use against him. He may also have been concerned that Congress might decide to look beyond the Veterans' Bureau and Fall's oil lease deals, in which case they might discover other rotten apples.

But two weeks after Forbes resigned, the Senate decided on its own to begin a full-scale investigation into the Veterans' Bureau. Two days after the announcement, Charles F. Cramer, general counsel of the Veterans' Bureau, committed suicide, adding more grist for the gossip mill. Cramer had been involved in many of Forbes' schemes and feared the exposure that would surely come.

More Shocking News

At about this time, Jess Smith, a close friend of Daugherty's, also committed suicide. It was reported that Smith was suffering from diabetes and depression. He shared a house with Daugherty and had an office in the Justice Department, although he was not on the government payroll. A mainstay of the Ohio Gang, Smith did whatever Daugherty asked him to do. As was later revealed, most of these "assignments" probably involved graft, bribery, or the use of Daugherty's powers as attorney general.

Sleepless Nights

In the spring of 1923, those close to the President noticed a drastic change in his manner. The pressures of his office, the scandals, and the betrayals by his friends had taken their toll. He could not sleep at night. His tolerant expression had hardened to "granite," one observer noticed. Those who came to the White House seeking political favors were advised to wear "nose guards and shin protectors."

At one point, Harding was heard to exclaim, "I have no trouble with my enemies. I can take care of my enemies all right. But my . . . friends . . . they're the ones that keep me walking the floors nights!"

Chapter 11
The Last Voyage

In the spring of 1923, as his administration continued to brave a stormy sea, Harding announced that he would embark upon a "Voyage of Understanding." He would travel by train and ship up to Alaska and be the first American President to set foot on the vast, virtually unspoiled wilderness.

Alaska was then a United States territory and not yet a state. As many as 33 government departments and bureaus claimed to have some say in how Alaska's natural resources should be developed. Harding thought his visit could help clear up some administrative bickering.

The embattled President also wanted to escape the politicians and the gossip-polluted air of Washington. The tremendously stressful events he had faced during the past year in office had affected his health. After a severe case of influenza in January, he had never fully regained his strength.

Only those closest to Harding knew he also suffered from a heart condition, which was rapidly getting worse. His blood pressure was abnormally high, and he could barely play six or seven holes of golf before he was too winded to continue. His heart ailment, combined with his worries, made it hard for him to sleep. Harding and his doctors thought the trip might be restful and restore his energy.

Despite his physical weariness, there was a new sense of purpose and determination in the President's manner. He seemed resolved to rise to the challenges of his presidency and overcome them. He wanted to run for re-election in 1924 and saw the trip as a good way to get back in touch with the voters. Inspired by this new sense of purpose, he was eager to get out among the American people and exchange ideas with them.

THE VOYAGE BEGINS AND ENDS

A large presidential party left Washington by train on June 20. Among the 65 guests traveling with the President and the First Lady were the Speaker of the House and three members of the Cabinet. There were also about 30 members of the press, Secret Service men, and other aides and personal friends. Doctor Sawyer, the Hardings' personal physician and another doctor were on the train, too. The First Lady was very concerned about her husband's health and made certain that at each stop the two doctors would have rooms near the President.

The route was planned to take the group west 1,500 miles through eight states, finally arriving at Tacoma, Washington. There, they would board a ship for passage to Alaska. Harding made about 14 speeches and several informal "whistle stops" along the way. He stopped to help cut grain on a farm in Kansas and even drove a tractor. As the train moved farther west, the crowds became larger and larger. There was a brutal heat wave in the West and his lips became blistered from speaking in the sun.

The President spoke about many domestic issues. But many of his speeches came back to his appeal for the United States to join the World Court. In Salt Lake City, he said: "I want America to have a spiritual ideal. I am seeking American sentiment in favor of an international court of justice. I want America to play her part in helping to abolish war."

President Harding on horseback in Zion National Park, July 4, 1923, one of the many stops he made while on his way to Alaska. The "Voyage of Understanding" was strenuous and Harding's health failing, but he still insisted on a demanding schedule. (Library of Congress.)

Harding Confides in Hoover

As the ship cruised north to Alaska, Harding seemed increasingly restless. Hoover later reported that "he insisted on playing bridge, beginning every day after breakfast . . . often until after midnight." He could not rest and walked the decks at night, long after his card-playing partners had gone to bed.

In a private moment, Harding asked Hoover what he would do if he were President and learned of some scandal in his government. Hoover immediately said he would make it public "and at least get credit for integrity on your side."

Harding then told Hoover that he learned of irregularities in the State Department involving Jess Smith. When he had sent for Smith and told him he would be arrested the following morning, Smith burned his papers and killed himself.

Hoover asked him if Daugherty was involved, but Harding would not answer.

The Voyage Ends

There were several stops in Alaska, and the President also spoke in Vancouver, Canada, on the return trip. He was the first American President to speak on Canadian soil. A crowd welcomed him in Vancouver, but even reporters remarked that he seemed exhausted.

On July 27, after speaking in Seattle, Harding became ill in the middle of the night. At first, the doctors thought he had eaten some tainted crab meat. When the train arrived in San Francisco on Sunday, July 29, he was brought to the Palace Hotel. It was clear to his doctors that he had suffered a cardiac collapse and also had pneumonia. The President refused to accept his doctors' advice, insisting that he would be back on his feet by Tuesday to give a major speech on foreign policy and the World Court.

The next few days Harding seemed to improve. His foreign policy address was released to the press by Herbert Hoover. By late Thursday, he was sitting up and chatting with a Secret Service man about the poor luck he had fishing in Alaska.

That night, Mrs. Harding read to the President. It was a complimentary newspaper article about him in *The Saturday Evening Post* called "A Calm Review of a Calm Man." He enjoyed it. "That's good," he told her. "Go on; read some more."

Mrs. Harding continued reading. Seconds later, the President made a gasping sound and slumped over in bed. Panicked, the First Lady ran from the room, calling for the doctors. The doctors attending Harding tried to revive him, but the attempt was futile. The President had died of massive heart failure.

The Return to Marion

The presidential train began the return trip to Washington draped in black. Harding's casket was placed so that it could be seen through the windows. The country was in deep shock; the crowds that came out to meet the train and pay their last respects were immense. One reporter commented that the crowds in Ohio were "so close together as to virtually suggest an aisle of mourners across the entire commonwealth."

Vice-President Calvin Coolidge had received a telegram from Daugherty the day of Harding's death and immediately took the presidential oath. When the train reached Washington on August 7, President Coolidge was at the station to meet Mrs. Harding.

Harding's casket laid in state in the Capitol rotunda on August 8. Over 35,000 people passed by the President's open casket; another 20,000 could not get in. Government officials voiced their grief at his passing. Even his political opponents felt a personal loss at his death.

On August 10, Warren Gamaliel Harding was buried in his beloved Marion, Ohio. "I have lost the best friend I ever had," his personal secretary, George Christian, told reporters, "and so has every American."

THE AFTERMATH

Formal hearings of the Veterans' Bureau investigation began on October 22, 1923, three months after Harding's death. Forbes was eventually tried and found guilty of defrauding the government.

Only two days later, the Senate hearings on Fall's oil leases were begun. The illegal dealings of Fall and the oil men, Sinclair and Doheny, caused a sensation in the press that was called the Teapot Dome scandal. The hearings dragged on into the spring of 1924. It was finally uncovered that Fall had received about $400,000 from both Sinclair and Doheny, paid in cash and securities.

After Harding's death, Daugherty remained as attorney general in Coolidge's administration. Then the Senate launched another full-scale investigation into Daugherty's actions at the Justice Department. The testimony of many witnesses revealed Jess Smith's criminal activities and connected Daugherty to bootlegging, oil deals, spying on government officials, failing to prosecute large companies on antitrust charges, and other crimes. When the investigating committee asked for Daugherty's files, he refused to surrender them, claiming it was a matter of national security. Pressured by Coolidge, he resigned. Daugherty later stood trial for defrauding the government but refused to testify. Due to the lack of evidence, the jury was not able to find him guilty.

The crimes these investigations uncovered cast a suspicious light over Harding's entire administration and, of course, upon Harding as well. However, there was never any evidence that he was connected in any illegal activities. Harding knew something of Smith's activities and perhaps even of Daugherty's. As his conversation with Hoover en route to Alaska might suggest, he may have been considering whether or not to expose Daugherty when he returned to Washington. But it is impossible to say for sure why Harding did not expose these men immediately and initiate legal action against them.

A Final Consideration

In considering Harding's presidency, it is important to note that his administration faced many difficult postwar problems, for which some very good solutions were provided. But Harding's accomplishments and his own personal integrity have been obscured by the greed and immorality of some of the people in his administration—men like Fall, Forbes, and Daugherty.

Probably Harding's greatest weakness as President was not a lack of intellect or leadership. He was not the first man—and certainly will not be the last—to enter the White House with a slim chance of being remembered as a great President. Ironically, Harding's most significant flaw turned out to be a trait he was very proud of—the loyalty and faith he showed his friends. The consequences were unfortunate and perhaps even tragic, both for the man who hoped to be remembered as America's best-loved President and for the American people he sincerely loved.

Bibliography

Boardman, Jr., Fon W. *America and the Jazz Age: A History of the 1920's*. New York: Walck, 1968. This very interesting book about the 1920s includes information about Harding and the social and political events before, during, and after his presidency.

Mee, Jr., Charles L. *The Ohio Gang: The World of Warren G. Harding, A Historical Entertainment*. New York: Evans, 1981. This book reads like an entertaining novel. It gives a colorful picture of the Hardings, their friends, and the political figures of the era. The author claims that all details are historically accurate; however, many details could be considered assumptions about events in Harding's life.

Murray, Robert K. *The Harding Era: Warren Harding and His Administration*. Minneapolis: University of Minnesota Press, 1969. A very detailed account of the activities and achievements of Harding's administration that also includes some biographical information. It is a little dry and the author's perspective is very sympathetic to Harding.

Russell, Francis. *The Shadow of Blooming Grove: Warren G. Harding and His Times*. New York: McGraw Hill, 1968. Many consider this book the best researched and most complete biography of Harding. It is well written, with many colorful details of Harding's life, and gives a balanced view of the subject.

Sinclair, Andrew. *The Available Man: Warren Gamaliel Harding*. New York: Macmillan, 1965. This is a well-respected biography that focuses on the reasons for Harding's successful rise to the presidency and his shortcomings as President.

Index

PRESIDENTS OF THE UNITED STATES

GEORGE WASHINGTON	L. Falkof	0-944483-19-4
JOHN ADAMS	R. Stefoff	0-944483-10-0
THOMAS JEFFERSON	R. Stefoff	0-944483-07-0
JAMES MADISON	B. Polikoff	0-944483-22-4
JAMES MONROE	R. Stefoff	0-944483-11-9
JOHN QUINCY ADAMS	M. Greenblatt	0-944483-21-6
ANDREW JACKSON	R. Stefoff	0-944483-08-9
MARTIN VAN BUREN	R. Ellis	0-944483-12-7
WILLIAM HENRY HARRISON	R. Stefoff	0-944483-54-2
JOHN TYLER	L. Falkof	0-944483-60-7
JAMES K. POLK	M. Greenblatt	0-944483-04-6
ZACHARY TAYLOR	D. Collins	0-944483-17-8
MILLARD FILLMORE	K. Law	0-944483-61-5
FRANKLIN PIERCE	F. Brown	0-944483-25-9
JAMES BUCHANAN	D. Collins	0-944483-62-3
ABRAHAM LINCOLN	R. Stefoff	0-944483-14-3
ANDREW JOHNSON	R. Stevens	0-944483-16-X
ULYSSES S. GRANT	L. Falkof	0-944483-02-X
RUTHERFORD B. HAYES	N. Robbins	0-944483-23-2
JAMES A. GARFIELD	F. Brown	0-944483-63-1
CHESTER A. ARTHUR	R. Stevens	0-944483-05-4
GROVER CLEVELAND	D. Collins	0-944483-01-1
BENJAMIN HARRISON	R. Stevens	0-944483-15-1
WILLIAM McKINLEY	D. Collins	0-944483-55-0
THEODORE ROOSEVELT	R. Stefoff	0-944483-09-7
WILLIAM H. TAFT	L. Falkof	0-944483-56-9
WOODROW WILSON	D. Collins	0-944483-18-6
WARREN G. HARDING	A. Canadeo	0-944483-64-X
CALVIN COOLIDGE	R. Stevens	0-944483-57-7

HERBERT C. HOOVER	B. Polikoff	0-944483-58-5
FRANKLIN D. ROOSEVELT	M. Greenblatt	0-944483-06-2
HARRY S. TRUMAN	D. Collins	0-944483-00-3
DWIGHT D. EISENHOWER	R. Ellis	0-944483-13-5
JOHN F. KENNEDY	L. Falkof	0-944483-03-8
LYNDON B. JOHNSON	L. Falkof	0-944483-20-8
RICHARD M. NIXON	R. Stefoff	0-944483-59-3
GERALD R. FORD	D. Collins	0-944483-65-8
JAMES E. CARTER	D. Richman	0-944483-24-0
RONALD W. REAGAN	N. Robbins	0-944483-66-6
GEORGE H.W. BUSH	R. Stefoff	0-944483-67-4

GARRETT EDUCATIONAL CORPORATION
130 EAST 13TH STREET
ADA, OK 74820